MEMORIES OF
THE CLIFF HOTEL

PAMELA LIND McCALLUM
NANCY MURRAY YOUNG

CONVERPAGE
23 Acorn Street
Scituate, MA 02066
www.converpage.com

To order additional copies contact:
CONVERPAGE
Email: pmccallum@comcast.net
Phone: 781-378-1996

Front Cover: **Panoramic photo** - Courtesy of The Scituate Historical Society
Back Cover: **Original Cliff Hotel Sign**, Rte. 3A and Henry Turner Bailey Road (top left)
Courtesy of Edward McCarthy, St. Augustine, Florida
Fire Photo (bottom center) Courtesy of Larry Niland, Scituate, Massachusetts

ISBN: 978-0-9858282-2-6

MEMORIES OF THE CLIFF HOTEL

This book is dedicated to my mother and father.

In memory of Alvin Lind (1928-2010) for teaching me
to cherish my hometown history and family.
I love and miss you every day, Dad.

With love to Geraldine Lind for supporting, assisting and
always being by my side for all my years in the publishing business.
I did it, Mom.

Pamela Lind McCallum

This book is dedicated to my parents.

In loving memory of my father, Gregg Murray (1915-1996),
a professional musician who played one summer
at The Cliff Hotel.

With love and appreciation to my mother, Lois Hurwitch Murray,
who grew up on Glades Road, just down the street
from The Cliff Hotel.

Their paths crossed. And the rest is history.

Nancy Murray Young

Table of Contents

INTRODUCTION

The fiery destruction of Scituate's Cliff Hotel in 1974 is a time capsule moment for many Town residents: we remember where we were when we learned of the fire that leveled Scituate's last grand hotel.

Those of us who had some personal connection to 'The Cliff' felt a deep sense of loss as memories of summer afternoons, junior proms and celebrity sightings rose like ghosts from the ashes.

From its beginning as a pleasant seaside vacation spot to its heyday as a resort for visiting celebrities, the hotel played an important role in Scituate – providing jobs, supporting commerce in the community, and offering an elegant venue for special events.

Yet, when Pam began to work on this project, she found that when she mentioned The Cliff Hotel, the most common response she heard was, "I remember the night it burned down..."

With this book, we have endeavored to tell a larger story of her legacy. Though many pieces of the past are long gone, we hope that we have captured the essence of her grandeur and secured her place in Scituate's history.

Pamela Lind McCallum
Nancy Murray Young
Scituate, Massachusetts, 2012

CLIFF HOTEL, NO. SCITUATE, MASS.

THE CUSHING FAMILY: FROM BOARDERS TO HOSTS

This "Historical Sketch of Early North Scituate, or Minot," by Daniel P. Sylvester, which was read at the 1927 annual meeting, offers a peek at the origins of the Cliff House:

"In the year 1837 my father, H.H. Sylvester, settled in this town. The town in those days differed much as we know North Scituate or Minot today ... It was a rare treat to see people in this vicinity in those days ... Not over a half dozen people would be seen all summer ... There were no roads - just pasture land and over this, one would have to drive to reach the beach or ocean front.

"My father was the first person on this beach to have the first two boarders, and they were a Mr. and Mrs. Cushing. They paid him $10.00 for their board and room. They stayed with him two weeks, so (at) that rate, they paid $2.50 apiece per week. He had a boat which he rented by the hour and one never used a boat over two hours at a time, the rate of 17 cents per hour.

> "The Cliff House was built by Mrs. Cushing. She let it (go), and it was idle for a long time.
>
> It was rebuilt by Mr. Summers, and he made it a great benefit to the Town of Scituate."

In 1961, Alan Howard, a student at Yale (and relative of the Cushing family), who was working at the Cliff Hotel, interviewed the Cushing's daughter for his thesis. Howard shared some of that information in the 8-17-61 issue of the South Shore Mirror:

"Overlooking beautiful Cohasset Green in a stately, white Colonial house, lives a charmingly spry lady not quite seventy-five years young. Her name is Mrs. Edward Souther, daughter of the original owners of the Cliff Hotel.

Thanks to some old letters, a diary, and Mrs. Souther's almost unfailing memory, we pieced together the fascinating story of the origin and development of one of New England's best-known resort hotels.

On December 1, 1895, Mrs. Mary Cushing, mother of Mrs. Souther and wife of prominent Boston lawyer, Louis T. Cushing, commissioned a certain Mr. Tibbets of Hull to begin work on the structure now known as the Cliff Hotel. Prior to that time there had been on the site a smaller building that was probably built sometime in the 1870s.

This house was owned by the Cushing family and was known as a very fashionable guesthouse called the Cliff House. Thus, one mystery surrounding the origin of the hotel is cleared; forever since its conception, the Cliff has been officially known as the Cliff Hotel and Cottages, but for some heretofore inexplicable reason has always been popularly called the Cliff House. Thanks to Mrs. Souther we now know that it was, indeed, the Cliff House nearly a century ago, and either out of nostalgia or just plain habit, people have referred to it as that ever since.

But it was this very same Cliff House that caused the Cushings a bit of consternation back in 1895, for they found it could be necessary to remove the old house in order to make way for the new hotel.

But no challenge was too great for the inimitable Mr. Tibbetts of Hull. He proposed the rather unique idea of cutting the house in half and moving it to the rear of the property. Today, both parts of the original structure are in use. One is a cottage on Cherry Lane called Grey Gables, the other, originally named Cherry Cottage, is now used to house the employees of the hotel.

Even before the turn of the century, Sunday dinner at the Cliff was a gathering of the fashionable and the sociable. But Mrs. Souther recalls a few notable differences from the Cliff of 1961. For one thing, Sunday dinner was in the afternoon, not the evening, and maids and children were not allowed into the dining hall. The buckboard, drawn by a handsome spotted grey and a sturdy bay, was used to meet guests from all over the country at the railroad station in North Scituate and bore little resemblance to the shiny new station wagon that now meets the guests.

Early every morning the watering cart would pass by to wet down the dusty road out front, now known as Ocean Ave.
Photo courtesy of Neil Murphy

An advertising circular around 1900 states: 'Best facilities for Bathing, Boating, and Fishing, Also Boarding and Livery Stable.' It goes on to say that, 'The furnishings and table are first class. Rates $2.50 to $3.00 per day, and special rates by the month or season.'

Then financial disaster struck the hotel, and the summer of 1904 was the last season it was operated by Mrs. Cushing."

ALTHOUGH WE FOUND VERY LITTLE INFORMATION about the years between 1904 and 1915 when Herbert Summers purchased the hotel, it appears that the property was overseen by the R.M. Morse group who leased it to professional managers.

June 21, 1912

The Cliff Hotel and Cottages, occupying one of the finest positions on the South Shore at North Scituate Beach, will open for guests June 28 under the able management of Edward Wiltbank, for many years past with the Hotel Chamberlin, Old Point Comfort, Va., one of the largest and finest hotels in the South.

Mr. Wiltbank has refurbished and redecorated the Cliff and Cottages and made numerous changes for the comfort of his guests and the prospects for a good season are excellent, over half the rooms in the hotel being already let to families for the season. A first class table under the personal direction of Mr. Wiltbank will be a feature and a new and attractive tearoom with French windows has been added. Professor Wyberlye's orchestra will begin concerts Sunday night June 30, and continue through the season. Every Sunday evening a special supper will be served of broiled live lobsters and wholesome seafood.

This item appeared in Floretta Vining's column in the "Scituate Light."
Mrs. Vining, of Hull, ran her own "Vining Syndicate" of papers on the
South Shore, which included the Scituate Light.

From Scituate Yesterdays, compiled by John Galluzzo for the
Scituate Historical Society, Scituate Mariner, June 23, 2012

THE CLIFF HOTEL
AND COTTAGES

MINOT'S LIGHT

HERBERT G. SUMMERS
PROPRIETOR

P. O. Address, Minot, Mass.   R. R. Station, North Scituate, Mass.

A New Owner, New Look, Greater Success

From the Boston Evening Transcript, June 12, 1915

Papers have passed in the sale of the Cliff House at North Scituate to Herbert G. Summers of the Charlesgate, who has had the property under contract for the last month. Extensive alterations are being made, and the house will open on Wednesday, June 30, for the season. Mr. Summers takes title from R.M. Morse, et als., trustees, to the hotel building of 100 rooms, seven cottages and eight acres of land fronting on the bay, opposite Minot's Light. A. Dudley Dowd negotiated the sale.

Town Report 1937

Summers became interested in the hotel business while stopping at the Mitchell House at North Scituate Beach, then operated by the late George G. Smith – whose daughter, Fanny, he married on June 24, 1907. He joined the staff at the Hotel Thorndike, Boston that year. In 1911, he took over the management of the Charlesgate Hotel, Boston, which he subsequently bought. He continued to operate the Charlesgate after purchasing the Cliff and ran both until 1937.

He became a civic leader as well as a business leader in Scituate: In 1921, he was elected to a 3-year term as selectman, assessor and "overseer of the poor." In 1929 he was elected to a three-year term on the advisory board. He was a 32nd degree Mason, Knight Templar and Shriner.

The Cliff properties, which grew and flourished under his guidance were the means of acquainting countless summer visitors from all over the United States and Canada, with Scituate.

SCITUATE WILL MISS THIS KINDLY AND BELOVED CITIZEN, BUT WILL NOT FORGET HIM. HIS LIFE AND WORK SPELLED HIS EPITAPH SIMPLY AND SINCERELY, WITH ONE WORD. SERVICE.

FROM THE 1937 SCITUATE TOWN REPORT DEDICATION

Summers was a skillful marketer

Having worked for two prominent Boston hotels, Herbert Summers knew the value of well-crafted promotional brochures with enticing descriptions and photographs.

The Cliff

NORTH SCITUATE
BEACH,
MASSACHUSETTS.

The Cottages

The cottages have all modern conveniences, including bathrooms, electric lights, open fireplaces and sanitary plumbing. They may be rented for the season thoroughly furnished for parties who prefer the quiet of an individual house to living in the hotel proper.

The Promenade in Front of the Hotel

The cement walk along the sea wall in front of the hotel affords a most delightful promenade and vantage point, from which to watch the activities on the beach during the bathing hour.

Bound Brook Bridge at North Scituate Station

From the hotel, fine motor roads lead to the famous Jerusalem Road. A few miles south is historic Plymouth, Daniel Webster's home in Marshfield, "The Old Oaken Bucket", and the old town of Scituate so closely connected with the Pilgrims. Close at hand is the Old Scituate Light, and to the northward, in full view from the hotel piazzas is the grim sentinel tower of Minot's Light, one of the most celebrated beacons in the world.

Adjacent Cottages and Glades Road

The hotel makes every effort to provide amusements for its guests, including dances given at frequent intervals, to which the neighboring cottagers are always welcome. Croquet, rowing, sailing, deep-sea fishing, beautiful walks and drives may be indulged in to their fullest extent.

Beach in the Summer

The beach, which lies less than twenty-five yards from the hotel, is one of the finest on the north Atlantic Coast and it has a stretch of hard white sand nearly two miles long. Its slope is so gradual that it makes an ideal and safe playground for children.

The Beach at Sunrise

The hotel has the best of automobile service, which can be furnished to guests at short notice. North Scituate, two miles distant is the railroad station, and is reached from Boston over the New York, New Haven and Hartford Railroad.   Automobiles meet every train.

The Glades

Within ten minutes walk from the hotel are the wonderful "Glades" containing over one hundred acres of woodland with delightful paths leading in all directions.

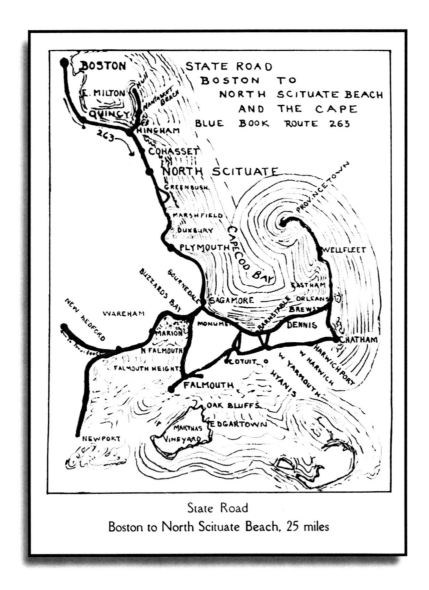

State Road
Boston to North Scituate Beach, 25 miles

The Lobby

We take much pains to see that this department of the hotel is kept up to a high standard. A dining room adjoins for nurses and children. The aim of the management is to make the hotel quiet and attractive, to encourage on the best people as patrons, and to give first class accommodation and service at moderate rates.

The Living Room

The well ventilated dining room is characterized by an excellent cuisine and efficient service. The first floor has two large parlors with smoking and writing rooms adjoining and a spacious lobby where informal dances are held. The sleeping rooms are large and airy, all having an outside exposure. Rooms may be arranged singly or en suite with or without baths.

The Hotel From the Water

The Cliff and Cottages are delightfully situated on a bluff, one of the most picturesque spots on the South Shore, commanding an uninterrupted view of the Atlantic from Cape Ann to Cape Cod.

Its approach is through a country of great historic interest, dotted with beautiful estates, and roads brought to a high state of efficiency, which afford automobilists a continual delight.

The Hatherly Golf Club is but two minutes' walk from the hotel. There are excellent tennis courts connected, and it has one of the best nine hole golf courses on the South Shore. On certain dates and under certain restrictions guests of the hotel may be allowed the privileges of the Club.

1935

THE TERRACE ROOM AT THE CLIFF HOTEL, NORTH SCITUATE BEACH, WILL OPEN FOR THE SEASON ON SATURDAY, JUNE 29TH, AND WILL BE OPERATED AS THE TERRACE CLUB, WITH A MEMBERSHIP LIMITED TO A SELECTED CLIENTELE.

MEMBERSHIP CARDS WILL BE ISSUED ON PRESENTATION OF THE ENCLOSED CARD OF INTRODUCTION TO THE MANAGEMENT.

AFTER JUNE 12TH, RESERVATIONS MAY BE MADE FOR THE OPENING AND MEMBERSHIP CARDS WILL BE ISSUED AT THE HOTEL.

Music by SAM   OPENING SEMI-FORMAL

Sea Gull Tea Room Before and After the Wreck, March,1916.

The Sea Gull Tea Room and Gift Shop is located on the grounds of the hotel where you will find many attractive articles for sale and where homemade dainties are served .

One of the interesting accommodations at the Cliff Hotel is the Sea Gull Cottage, part of the super structure of the barge Ashland that was washed ashore after the barge went down with all hands during a violent winter storm that swept the area in March 1916. The super structure was salvaged and later converted to a nautical cottage. The original flooring and the beams with original inscriptions are still intact. Visitors are invited to inspect the relic of the sea.

History of the Tea Room

Courtesy of United States Congressional Serial Set
U.S.Government Printing Office
Schooner-Barges "Ashland" and Kohinoor" in Tow of Steamship "Swatara"

These barges, the second and third, respectively, of a tow of three barges were proceeding from Boston for Philadelphia, when about 5:30 p.m., March 3, 1916 the hawser between the first and second barges parted, setting the second and third barges adrift. The *Swatara* swung around for the purpose of picking up the two barges, but the sea was found to be too rough to attempt this with one barge still in tow. The *Swatara*, therefore, returned to Boston, where the first barge was anchored. She then proceeded to sea to look for the Ashland and the Kohinoor, but a heavy snowstorm had set in and she was compelled to return to Boston. Early in the morning of March 4, 1916 the weather cleared and the *Swatara* returned to take up the search.

The master of the *Ashland* attempted to sail to safe anchorage upon being set adrift with the *Kohinoor*. Owing to the severe gale she was unable to make headway with the other barge, so the *Kohinoor* was signaled to cast off his hawser. The gale increasing, the *Ashland* sagged down to leeward, when the master let go anchors. The barge dragged her anchors until she struck a submerged reef and at daybreak, March 4, she was discovered lying to leeward of Smith Rock, east of Minot's Light, where she broke up. The crew of the barge was rescued from the wreckage by the life-saving crew of North Scituate Life Saving Station. After casting off from the Ashland the Kohinoor broke up, with the loss of her entire crew of four men.

The vessels, both in ballast, were valued at $6,188.37 for the Ashland and $3,404.80 for the Kohinoor, and are both total losses.

This casualty was investigated by the local inspectors of steam vessels at Boston, who preferred charges against the master of the *Swatara*, the towing steamer, for negligence, unskillfulness, and endangering life. On trial he was found guilty and his license was suspended for six month.

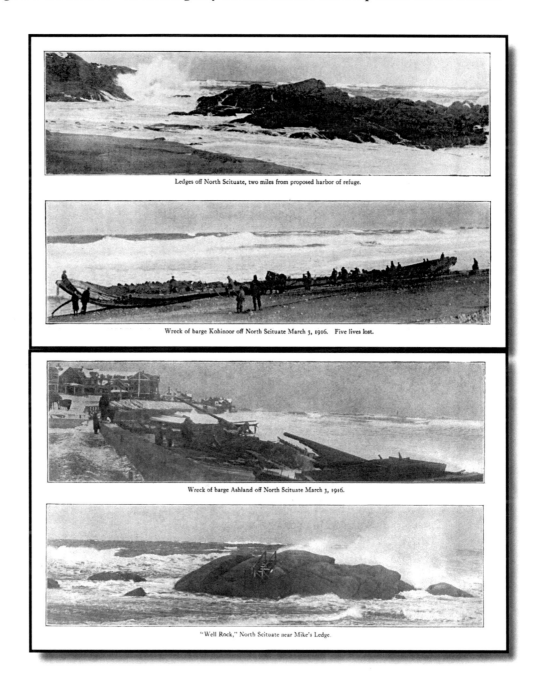

Ledges off North Scituate, two miles from proposed harbor of refuge.

Wreck of barge Kohinoor off North Scituate March 3, 1916.   Five lives lost.

Wreck of barge Ashland off North Scituate March 3, 1916.

"Well Rock," North Scituate near Mike's Ledge.

Floor Plans of Cliff Hotel and Cottages

The location of the Cliff Hotel and Cottages upon an eminence above both the ocean and the surrounding country, effectively captures the prevailing southwest winds for the comfort and delight of guests during hot weather. The nights of the hottest days are rendered comfortable by the refreshing night winds.

Rooms in the hotel may be had with or without bath, singly or in suites of two or more, with or without living-room.

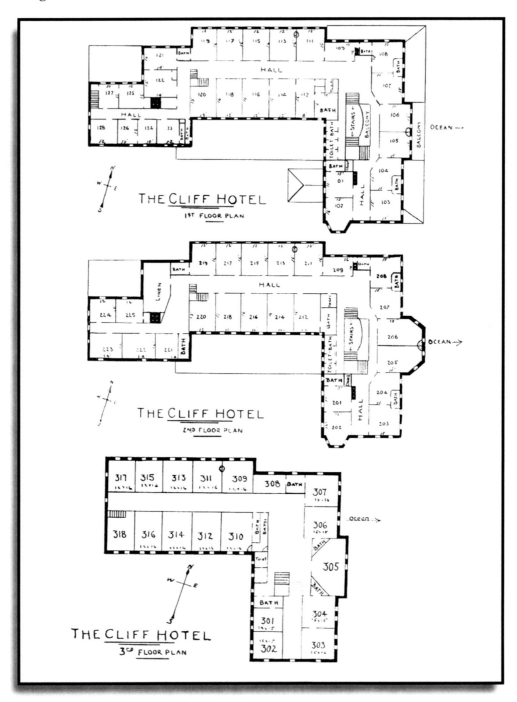

At the request of the guests who make reservations for more extended stays, suites of rooms in the cottages including living-room, bedrooms and bath can be arranged.

Correspondence is invited by the management concerning any particulars of the service offered its guests by the Cliff Hotel and Cottages or by the Charlesgate Hotel, Boston.

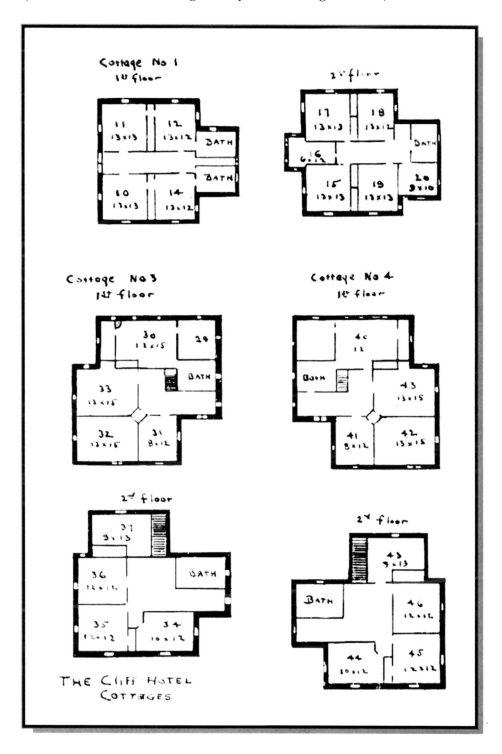

THE CLIFF AND COTTAGES are delightfully situated at North Scituate Beach, in the heart of Puritan New England, adjoining the fascinating South shore and highway, between Boston, Plymouth and Cape Cod. Here the visitor will find a wealth of historic interest and a combination of seashore and country of most unusual charm.

The hotel itself is high above the beach upon a terraced embankment fronted by a seawall and promenade. The guest takes great pleasure in its carefully-planned service; appetizing food fresh from the nearby farms and ocean; broad piazzas; comfortable and attractive lounging rooms; open fireplaces; clean, fresh sleeping rooms, and with daily concerts and informal dances, there is a pervasive feeling of friendliness, comfort and enjoyment.

THE COTTAGES are designed primarily for those who prefer the quiet of an individual house to living in a hotel, or for families with small children. The rooms can be arranged en suite of living room, three or four bedrooms and bath.

For those who desire to indulge in them, The Cliff provides ample facilities for the several sports; the excellent golf courses of the Scituate and Hatherly Country Clubs are both near and, under certain rules and restrictions are open to the guests of the hotel. Tennis courts are available and a stable of fine saddle horses, with riding school in conjunction is located within walking distance. An added attraction is a playground for children on the grounds of the hotel.

Address all correspondence to HERBERT G. SUMMERS, The Charlesgate, 35 Beacon St., Boston, Mass. After June 1st, The Cliff, No. Scituate Beach - Minot P.O. - Mass.

R.R. Station North Scituate, Mass., on N.Y., N.H. & H. Railroad - 25 miles from South Station, Boston. Automobiles meet every train.

THE CLIFF HOTEL. NORTH SCITUATE BEACH. MASS.

"Gateway to Cape Cod"
CLIFF HOTEL and COTTAGES
North Scituate Beach,
Minot P. O., Mass.
On Its Own Private Beach.

THE WRITING ROOM

Spectra-Color
POSTCARD
REPRODUCED FROM NATURAL COLOR PHOTOGRAPH

I am here at the Cliff
And I'm feeling as if
Every worry and care
    had vacated
A sky, and a beach.
And a "Bar" within reach
I surely am well
    "Scituated"

Address

MEMORIES OF
THE CLIFF HOTEL

THE BRAZILIAN FAMILY YEARS   1942 - 1970

My mother and father bought the hotel in the early 1940s and had no hotel experience. I was in the second grade. My father was a struggling attorney and my mother was his legal secretary.

During the first few years, my father would work seven days a week and would help people with their tax returns to make extra money. I remember my mother would paint all the rooms during the winter months.

My father would drive to Quincy with all of the laundry and I would go with him just to make sure he wouldn't fall asleep.

He was the hardest working man I ever knew. He was an inspiration and taught me to be a hard worker throughout my life.

Aram Brazilian, Jr., 2012

The following excerpts from Aram Brazilian, Sr.'s autobiography, *Aram*, provide a rare and intimate portrait of the hotel's years as a world-class vacation destination under his family's stewardship.

We are grateful to Aram Brazilian, Jr. for so generously sharing these photos, articles and memories for this publication.

Many of the photographs were taken by noted Scituate photographer Rudy Mitchell.

" *The Purchase ...*

Through a client, I was informed that the Cliff Hotel, a long established resort hotel on the Atlantic Ocean was for sale. I had a dream, some day I would own a resort hotel... I made an appointment with the owner, Richard Summers ... in September, 1942, I drove to North Scituate, Mass. where the hotel was located.

The main building's first floor was the cocktail lounge, which after renovation, I named The Brazilian Bamboo Lounge. On the same floor ... a modern coffee shop was added.

In the rear on the same floor were the bakery, boiler room, large walk-in chest, liquor and grocery storeroom.

The second floor was the main entrance to the hotel lobby. It contained the registration desk, offices, the gift shop, three reception rooms, and the main dining room with its side dining room for private parties. A large veranda faced the ocean and was converted into an attractive ocean front breakfast room. The next three floors of the hotel were the bedrooms, some with private bath, a few with connecting baths. On the south side of the hotel facing the ocean was a large three-story frame building, used as an annex to the hotel.

In back of it was the second cottage, known as the Summers' Cottage, because the owners lived there. There were also Cottages Three and Four, known as the Twin Cottages, constructed alike, two story frame houses containing full facilities for the occupancy of a large family. Facing Cherry Lane was the Lodge, later added to the property to accommodate Mrs. Summers' parents the Smiths. The Employees Cottage, facing Cherry Lane, a three-story frame building housed the female employees. The beautiful path to the cottages was lined up with graceful poplar trees and a variety of rose bushes and flowers.

After the tour, Richard Summers told me that hotel had been partially opened during the past season, because of war restrictions, and he was managing the hotel for pleasure after the death of his father, Herbert Summers. Herbert had operated the hotel for twenty-seven years for high-class carriage clientele.

1943 Hurricane

The treacherous Hurricane of 1943 hit us the closing days of our first season in the Cliff Hotel. We still had 40 guests in the hotel. Our bartender, Joe Callahan had experience hurricanes in Florida and knew how to cope with it. He took charge and provided protective measures by reinforcing doors and shutters. However, water coming through oceanfront bedroom windows exhausted our supply of towels ... 42 poplar trees were uprooted. The electricity was shut off for two days, forcing us to use candlelight. Good thing our kitchen was equipped with gas ranges, enabling us to serve meals.

We experienced another devastating hurricane that kept us without lights for two weeks in mid-season with a full house. Imagine our fear and sleepless nights when we had to provide our guests with a candle stuck in a beer bottle on their way to their bedroom. In spite of the inconveniences, the guests did not check out and took it with good humor and cheerfulness. Our hotel was considered safer than any other building in the neighborhood and it provided refuge to many neighbors.

Cocktail Parties

On Monday evenings, all the guests, by written invitation, attended the Manager's Cocktail Party by the poolside. The orchestra played during the one-hour party and as a frivolity, one of the orchestra members would be thrown into the pool with a dummy instrument.

Warm friendships were created. At the end the orchestra would lead the guests to the main dining room for dinner and the newly acquainted friends would pull their tables together and continue the merriment and dances.

Sunday Buffet

The Cliff Hotel Sunday Buffet became an institution. Customers came from far and near and got in line and, at times, waited for an hour in order to enjoy the buffet replenished with fifty seven varieties, including unlimited helpings of freshly caught Scituate lobster. Tip O'Neill, our House speaker, was one of the frequent guests of our Sunday Buffet.

The Brazilian Bamboo Lounge

The Brazilian Bamboo Lounge had become the most popular lounge on the South Shore. Six nights a week, the live music provided entertainment and dancing of the highest quality.

The Surfside Five* played in the lounge for four seasons. They came back year after year by popular demand. *(*Editor's note: Soon redubbed The Cliffside Five).*

To promote interest and enjoyment, we had attractive programs for guests of the hotel and outside patrons. One of the most popular programs was our employees' show that we used to put on twice every season. The performers were college boys and girls, employed for the season.

The most popular song at the hotel was "My Wild Irish Rose," since most of the North Scituate Beach residents were Irish and the beach was called the Irish Riviera. On Friday and Saturday nights, we had to engage a policeman to stand at the entrance to govern the overflow crowd.

Coffee Shop

The hotel's Coffee Shop was a very successful operation, especially when we modernized and equipped it with fast service equipment. I still miss the most delicious hamburgers the Coffee Shop was noted for, and it used to draw hundreds of non-guest customers from the beach. Also, our guests were on their own for lunch, hence a good coffee shop was a must.

Clam Bakes

The Cliff Hotel had a fine reputation of serving real New England clambakes. Every day in the months of June and September, which was our off-season period, I used to book an outing every day for insurance companies and banks as well as class reunions and various business organizations. One year, John Hancock Insurance Company, for three consecutive Thursdays, brought groups of five hundred employees for a New England Clam Bake outing. We rented tables and chairs and set them up outdoors on the hotel grounds, overlooking the open Atlantic.

Another memorable Clam Bake was held for the New England Fashion Manufacturers convention in Boston. We served 1000 guests who arrived from Boston in special buses. This was a challenge for me to live up to.

We hired 48 college girls to act as waitresses. I ordered brand new uniforms for them to wear that did not arrive until one hour before serving time. You can imagine the anxiety we all went through, including the poor excited waitresses, who had to pick their right size. It was a sight to be proud of, 48 young girls in crisp bright uniforms carrying trays of red lobsters, clams and corn. Our cocktail lounge and three outside bars employed a dozen bartenders. The income from the open bars broke all records."

There was a time when the town wanted to take 5 acres behind the hotel by eminent domain for a parking lot. In the winter prior to that time the entire area was completed submerged in water. I took pictures and brought them to the town meeting. The town never took the land. It would have cost them thousands of dollars to fill in the area.

My father purchased 1-1/2 acres on the corner of Route 3A and Henry Turner Bailey Road just so he could put the Cliff Hotel sign there.

Aram Brazilian, Jr., 2012

The Boston Globe

Feature Story: July 10, 1955
Boston Sunday Globe

Cliff Hotel Offers Relaxation and Fun

One of New England's foremost Summer resorts, the Cliff Hotel and Cottages, situated on the oceanfront in the fashionable North Scituate area is enjoying its 63rd season of operation.

Owned and managed by Aram Brazilian, the resort with its wonderful seacoast setting offers unexcelled facilities for rest and relaxation. Its accommodations are luxurious yet homelike, with every room equipped with private bath and telephone. All outside rooms

have an ocean view. There are large suites available or entire cottages on the grounds. There are a few one-bedroom apartments with living room, kitchenette and bath.

Cliff Hotel guests can be assured of activities galore, both indoors and outdoors. There is dancing nightly in the resort's romantic Brazilian Bamboo cocktail lounge or on the open-air deck to the strains of Dick Parent's orchestra. Bingo, cards, community singing, movies, talent night with prizes, rumba contests, theatre night and free transportation to the famous South Shore Players' Summer Theatre at nearby Cohasset, are included in the activities.

Guests can enjoy swimming and sun bathing on a beautiful sandy beach, picturesque walks, golf and tennis at the exclusive Hatherly Country Club, only five minutes' walk from the hotel, where hotel guests are accorded membership privileges.

There is also deep-sea fishing, cycling, ping-pong, croquet, horseshoes, archery and yachting.

One of the interesting accommodations at the Cliff Hotel is the Sea Gull Cottage, part of the super structure of the barge Ashland that was washed ashore after the barge went down with all hands during a violent winter storm that swept the area in March 1914.

The super structure was salvaged and later converted to a nautical cottage. The original flooring and the beams with original inscriptions are still intact. Visitors are invited to inspect the relic of the sea.

June 9 1957 - Famous Resort - Cliff Hotel Celebrating 15th year under Brazilian

One of New England's foremost summer resorts, the Cliff Hotel and Cottages, situated on the oceanfront in the fashionable North Scituate area, is celebrating its 15th anniversary under the same ownership and management.

Owned and operated by Aram Brazilian, Boston attorney, the resort with its seacoast setting offers unexcelled facilities for rest, fun and relaxation. Its accommodations are luxurious yet homelike, with every room equipped with private bath and telephone. All outside rooms have an ocean view. There are large suites available or entire cottages on the grounds.

Guests can enjoy swimming and sun bathing on a beautiful sandy beach. They may also relax and sunbathe while enjoying a cocktail on the Deck in front of the hotel overlooking the ocean. Guests returning this year will be pleased with the resplendent new Brazilian Bamboo Room. This popular lounge rendezvous has been air-conditioned and completely re-decorated. A new oval bar with modern foam rubber armrests have been installed. Here dancing may be enjoyed nightly.

The Cliff Hotel is justly famous for its excellent cuisine prepared by the best chefs available, and specializes in lobster, seafood's and other New England delicacies. Its Sunday night buffets have been the talk of the South Shore for years. Fifty-seven varieties of food delicacies have been dreamed up to delight each guest. The buffet is served from 6 p.m. to 8 p.m. each Sunday night

In June and July we held big banquets. Buses would pull up with hundreds of people. We served lobsters, chowder and chicken … delicious.

On Monday nights we would have cocktail parties from 5:00 to 7:00 and then everyone would move into the dining room. Monday nights were louder than usual.

Aram Brazilian, Jr., 2012
(Pictured, right, with Aram, Sr., center, and the executive chef)

 **"News Notes"**

Aram Brazilian, Sr. combined his pride in the Cliff Hotel and his way with words to create "Cliff Notes," a regular feature in local weekly papers. With its friendly tone and interesting stories about hotel guests and activities, the column kept the hotel front and center throughout each season – and, fortunately for us, preserved much of the hotel's history.

 " *I am glad that I saved copies of my News and Notes that appeared in the South Shore Mirror…* They became popular with guests, neighbors and employees. We would receive protests if we interrupted it a week or two. Our readers had become followers of our activities and interested to know all about our family members, children's schooling and all about the stars staying in the hotel.

August 3, 1961

One of the Highlights of the summer season is the Sunday night buffet served from 6 p.m. on….at the Cliff Hotel in North Scituate. Featuring seafood's of all kinds, as well as gourmet dishes from huge chafing dishes, this cool ocean front spot has become the Mecca for Sunday night diners from most everywhere.

Thursday, August 3, 1961   South Shore Mirror

August 23, 1962

The 1962 summer season is rapidly approaching its end, but there is still time to enjoy the fabulous Sunday night buffet at the Cliff Hotel.

If you are one of those who have been meaning to come all season, don't put it off any longer. Come over next Sunday and bring some friends along. Why not make a party of it? Labor Day, Sunday the 2nd will be the last one for our popular buffet. And you have two more weeks in which in which to enjoy the versatile Cherry Brothers and the 5-piece Cliff Dwellers, who entertain nightly in our Brazilian Bamboo Lounge.

We're still getting congratulations from our friends and guests on our 20th anniversary, which we have observed this year. Did you know that the Cliff Hotel has been a popular resort since 1899?

Congressman Thomas O'Neil of Cambridge and his family are our guests this week and we are proud to have this prominent family again this year. Congressman O'Neil is here for the Tobin Memorial Golf Tourney to be held this weekend.

Many of our guests this summer have commented on the special effort we are exerting to make this a memorable season. There's a reason for it.

Monday night in the dining room one of our long-time guests buttonholed me and said in effect- What goes on here? You seem to be going all out this year to make your guests happy. The Sunday buffet surpasses even those of other memorable summers, you have outstanding entertainers in the Cherry Brothers and Cliff Dwellers' orchestra, you have redecorated the Bamboo Lounge and your staff is outstanding.

This, of course, is music to our ears and we're glad to let you in on the secret. This is the 20th year that the Cliff Hotel has been operated by the Brazilian family and we decided before the season opened that we would try to make it something pretty special.

Our old friends will recall that we bought the Hotel in 1942, during the war, and converted what had been a White Elephant into one of the top resort hotels in New England. We are proud of our success here and we are grateful to the ever-growing number of people who come back season after season to make this success possible.

Last night we were hosts to some 200 Navy Reserve Fliers and their ladies from the South Weymouth Naval Air Station. We are still accepting reservations for outings and other functions after Labor Day and I am glad to tell you that the Scituate Dance Club will hold two Fall dances here.

June Carroll, glamorous star of stage and screen, has been a guest at the hotel with three or four children during her engagement at the Music Circus where she appears this week in the role made famous by Ethel Merman in "Gypsy."

South Shore News, Summer, 1962

CLIFF *hotel* "News Notes" *August 31, 1962*

Whee! What a rush of business!

Last Sunday evening our fabulous buffet attracted the largest crowd of the season and ...we regret to say... some had to be turned away.

We directed those we couldn't accommodate to two good eating places not far distant, where at one a hostess was heard to say: "It's a good thing the Cliff ran out of food."

This Sunday we will present the last buffet of the 1962 season and Chef Willis Gates is planning an extra special buffet. Incidentally, his ice carvings have won much favorable comment all summer.

Among the many guests who enjoyed the buffet Sunday we saw Congressman Thomas O'Neill with a large party of friends; Probate Court Judge Frederick V. McMenimen; Mr. and Mrs. Arthur Gartland (he's the Boston School Committeeman), and Mr. and Mrs. Roger J. Gardner of Collier Ave., Scituate. We were also pleased to welcome Chairman Lester Gates and Jackson Bailey of the Scituate Board of Selectmen, and their charming wives.

We are planning a gala evening in the Bamboo Lounge Sunday night, which will be the last of the season for the very talented Cherry Brothers and the popular music makers, the Cliff Dwellers. The lounge will be gaily decorated in New Year's Eve fashion. There will be prizes and favors and a Talent Night contest. After midnight there will be dancing. Why not come over and join the fun? You will be welcome!

Such is fame. Recently we took our shoes to a local cobbler for repair. It was our first visit so we identified our self as the owner of the Cliff Hotel. For an instant there was no reaction, then: "Oh, that's the place where Zsa Zsa Gabor stayed." We have been operating the Cliff for twenty years, but it was the one visit by Zsa Zsa that impressed our friend.

I remember when the pool was built. It was one of the first hotels in the state with a pool. They brought a crane in to put up the walls. There were 3 huge tanks in the basement that were part of the filter system. We had to fill each tank with sand pail by pail.
The pool was 25' by 50'. I had to repaint the walls every year. It took 24 hours to fill.

Aram Brazilian, Jr., 2012

Fashion shows, beauty contests and parties by the pool were hallmarks of summers at the Cliff. Here several young women register for the 1961 Miss Scituate Contest. Photo courtesy of Barbara Kane, former employee.

CLIFF *hotel* "News Notes" *July 11, 1963*

We have received many comments from our guests regarding the attractive appearance of our building since Fred Dorr and his crew did such a fine painting job.

Many have taken advantage of our Cabana Club membership offer and we are pleased to announce that the quota for this season has been filled. For those who were disappointed, we suggest that you apply early next season.

The moonlight splash party held last week was a great success and a gala affair. The Cliff Side Five from our Bamboo Lounge serenaded the Cabana Club members and hotel guests with Hawaiian tunes and their inimitable folk songs. The tantalizing aroma of the wiener roast and music filled the air. Needless to say, the youngsters of all ages had the time of their lives. I am pleased that the Cliff Side Five have won such general acclaim in so short a period. Their folk singing and versatile dance music is heard seven nights a week in the Bamboo Lounge.

Something new has been added at the Cliff Hotel this season. Our Oriental Gift Shop, containing many gift items selected by your hosts on our around-the-world tour last fall is popular with our guests and South Shore residents who enjoy browsing there.

We were pleased to see that more than half of the patrons at our famous buffet last Sunday evening were other than hotel guests. More and more, this popular Sunday night feature is attracting South Shore residents and summer folks who have found this a delightful way to dine on a summer evening. Why don't you drop in next Sunday and bring your friends or out of town guests? They will thank you for it.

July 23, 1964

Last Sunday Mrs. Brazilian and I made a hurried trip to Idlewild at Manomet Bluffs which is owned and managed by our son, Aram Jr. to attend a reception for my cousin Leon Demercian from Sao Paulo, Brazil. More than 100 attended including many of Leon's maternal relatives.

We rushed back to North Scituate in time to put the finishing touches on the Sunday night buffet, which had its largest attendance of the season. Our chef did an outstanding job again and many new items were added to the buffet table.

It gives me a lot of pleasure to extend congratulations to Miss Beth LaDue, who on Friday was crowned queen of the Massachusetts Lobster Festival at Marshfield. She is a lovely Scituate girl who is being squired these days by our popular pool lifeguard Bill Hunter. They certainly make a handsome pair.

I must not forget to mention that the Cliffside Five is still packing 'em in at the Bamboo Lounge seven nights a week.

As usual our guest list contains the names of many prominent people. Among them this week is the Rev. Adrian P. O'Leary of Brookline, visiting his mother who is here for the season; Mr. and Mrs. F.L. Quinlan of Roslindale; T. Robert Sullivan of Brookline, father of Judge Robert Sullivan of the State Superior Court; and Dr. and Mrs. S. B. Kelleher of Arlington.

I am pleased to announce that the Sixth Annual Fashion Show of the Chris'ter Club of St. Christine's Church, Marshfield, will be held in our dining room August 12 at 8:00 p.m. Mrs. Alfred D. Erickson of Marshfield Hills is in charge of the event. Clothes from Mr. Joseph of Hanover will be displayed by live models.

The smiling young lady who seats guests in the dining room is Miss Geraldine Murray of Newton, who started the season as a waitress but has now been named hostess. She is a student at the Newton College of Sacred Heart.

Our head room clerk this season is Miss Nell Jennings Cox, one of many southern girls on our staff. The daughter of a minister, she is a student at Meredith College, Raleigh, North Carolina.

Exact date not available: 1965

During our popular Sunday buffet this week we noticed some old friends of the Cliff Hotel and the Brazilians, Judge and Mrs. John V. Mahoney, and seated with them were Mr. and Mrs. John Burns.

At another table were Mr. and Mrs. Daniel Griffin and their daughter. Mr. Griffin was a leading figure in the Brinks robbery investigation as a member of the F.B.I. The Griffin's daughter Barbara will be remembered by some of you as our dining room hostess two years ago. It was here that she met her husband Joseph Kane, who was also an employee of the hotel that year.

Also among the house guests were Mr. and Mrs. Joseph W. Shea of Washington, D.C., with Father Linehan and Dr. Francis J. West, Jr. Mr. Shea is secretary to the Federal Trade Commission in Washington.

Photo courtesy of former employee Richard Darling, who is in the bottom row, second from the left!

Our efficient headwaiter this season has been Frederic S. Underhill who last year was a waiter here. He resides in Brookline with his parents. I was impressed with his work last season and offered him the headwaiter position. I'm glad to report that he has more than justified the confidence that I had in him.

Most of our waitresses and many of the other personnel on our staff are college students. Represented this year are students from Simmons, University of Massachusetts, Baylor University, Florida State, Regis College, Florida Southern College, Beaver College, Harvard and Boston University. Our bus boy is from Notre Dame College.

I am happy and proud to state that our staff this year has been most co-operative, loyal, and efficient, winning many praises from our guests for their courteous service. Now that the season is almost over, and they will soon be returning to their classes, I wish to thank them most sincerely and offer them an open invitation to return next season.

Last Monday evening at our customary poolside cocktail party we had the pleasure of entertaining 14 members of the Cohasset Subscription Dance Club headed by Mr. and Mrs. William H. Reardon, Jr. They are responsible for booking the Club's Fall Dance here October 25.

This Saturday we play host to a wedding reception for Janice Prosser, daughter of Mr. and Mrs. Everett W. Prosser, 41 Ridge Road, Marshfield, who will be married to David Leland. After hearing our Cliff Side Five in the Bamboo Lounge they engaged them to play for the reception.

July 30, 1964

Our Sunday night buffet, which I originated 21 years ago, is being greatly appreciated by our hotel guests. It is outstanding in every way, and is a treat that cannot be duplicated anywhere else in this area. It is served every Sunday from 6 to 9 p.m. and includes two hot dishes – juicy, tender Roast Beef, and Virginia Fried Chicken; many varieties of other dishes, salads and desserts, to the count of "57." All you can eat for $3.50 – Children $2.00.

This week, more than any so far, has been Homecoming Week here at the Cliff. So many of our guests who have made this their permanent summer home, have returned. To mention a few: Mr. and Mrs. Richard Allen, of Riverdale, New York; Mr. and Mrs. Cornelius Duggan of Watertown, Mass. and their two sons, one of whom is a cadet at the Air Force School in Colorado; Dr. and Mrs. J.M. Wilkinson Jr. and children from Summit, New Jersey; Mr. and Mrs. Frank Paradis and children of Arlington, Mass.; and Mr. and Mrs. John Yovicsin and children of Framingham, Massachusetts are again visiting. Mr. Yovicsin is head football coach at Harvard.

Any day you drive by, you will see many of our guests taking advantage of our swimming pool. It is a beautiful spot – and most comfortable on these hot mid-summer days.

The Cliffside Five continue to entertain seven nights a week at the Bamboo Lounge. This well-known group has "sell-out" popularity. Come early – stay late, and enjoy the fun!

Elsie and Aram, Sr., on the front terrace.

NORTH SCITUATE BEACH

"News Notes"

It is good to have the month of June behind us with its busy schedule of conventions, banquets, outings, clambakes and wedding receptions.

With the arrival of July, we enter our regular resort season and it is a daily pleasure to greet former guests who have come again to their "summer home." The Hotel's social program is in full swing the Cabana Club, cocktails and fashion shows by the poolside, moonlight splash parties for guests and members of the Cabana Club, the Bamboo Lounge with its Champagne Night, its Amateur Night and our most popular Cliff Side Five minus One pleasing our guests nightly.

Season's first Sunday Night Buffet got off to a great start with our new chef, Richard Southern and his crew, Leo Conlon and Lenace Prudhomme, doing an outstanding job. Of course our next one falls on Fourth of July and I promise you a Buffet table to reflect our greatest day, the Day of our Independence - God Bless America.

Why not treat your out of town guests to our famous Buffet? The price is $3.75, lobster and hot roast beef is included in the 57 varieties.

This summer we are introducing a smart new Sportswear Shop - The Village Trader - from Chestnut Hill, Mass., owned and operated by Jane and Dick McFarland. They are featuring some unusually attractive styles from such well-known houses as John Meyer of Norwich, Sue Brett, David Crystal, Craig-Craely, Cole of California and many others. They have Dresses - Suits - Blouses - Skirts - Slacks - Shorts - Bathing Suits, etc. A complete line of Misses' and Juniors Sportswear. In addition, some of these are their own original designs made up in their exclusive fabrics - and no charge for alterations.

In my last week's column, I mentioned our brand new Coffee Shop that was getting the finishing touches for the Ribbon Cutting Ceremony which will take place Thursday, July 1 at 6 p.m. Our Town Fathers have been invited to do the Ribbon Cutting. Representative Lester Gates will honor us with is presence. The Scituate Chamber of Commerce will be represented, so will the Quincy Ledger, The South Shore Mirror and The Scituate Herald. Mr. William Gardner, the architect and Mr. Stephen Peters, president of Interstate Fabrications, designers and manufacturers of all equipment will also be present.

This is going to be a hot summer, 3 more memberships to our Swimming Pool will complete the quota!

In closing may I wish you all a safe and happy Fourth of July.

Your host,
Aram Brazillian
South Shore News,
July 1, 1965

July 20, 1967

I have a lot to be thankful for on my 25th anniversary as owner manager of this fine New England hostelry, Last Tuesday night our Town Fathers granted the Cliff Hotel license to dance on Sundays in the Bamboo Lounge. The present board with its new Chairman Mr. J. Russell Harper will accomplish the faith and expectations placed by the residents of Scituate to promote this fine South Shore Resort Town.

The Pavement Narrows is the name of this year's orchestra, and their popularity has already equaled that of our Cliff-side Five that enjoyed four years of tremendous popularity. Three of the members are from Harvard and the fourth from MIT; they go by the individual names of David Ament, the leader, who plays piano and rhythm guitar; John Altman, drums; Jim Rosokoff, bass guitar, and David Altman, lead guitar.

On this Anniversary year we are also blessed with a grandson, Aram III, whose christening took place last Thursday, which happened to be my birthday – occasion for double celebration by my family. All my five sisters from Maine, R.I. and Mass. were present. My daughter Gail came all the way from Los Angeles with her four-year-old daughter Laura; she wrote the following poem wishing me a Happy Birthday:

"This is your life Dad"

Many years from Sao Paulo
Brazil came
A young Brazilian who was to
achieve much fame
He cut meat and owned stations
For gas
And through hard work the law
Exam he did pass
He set up a practice and
Many clients did defend
And loving his cute secretary
In the end
He married her and they had
3 kids
Whose accomplishments raised
A few eyelids -
He put them all through college
And such

And now has grandchildren he
Loves very much
"The Cliff" has been your life
For 25 years
Which, you've made successful
Through blood, sweat and tears
Today's your Birthday – 39
We're told -
So relax and be honored if we
May be so bold
You're loved and cherished by
One and all
So to put it simply......
HAVE A BALL!!!

Love, Gail, Ray and Laura

August 21, 1968

Two weeks until Labor Day Weekend. Where has the summer gone? We plan to keep the Cliff open until the end of October this year, as our function business is the busiest in 26 years under the Brazilian Family.

Our Dining Room will remain open to guests and transients until September 15, and then we will just rent our rooms "Motel Style" for the remainder of September and October.

Next Sunday, August 25, we will entertain the Keydata Corp, of Watertown, 250 in number, for a Clambake. The weekend of September 6-7, North Quincy High School 20th Year Class Reunion will be making the Cliff their headquarters. On Monday, September 9, the Scituate Chamber of Commerce will hold their monthly meeting with dinner served on "The Deck" overlooking the ocean. Tuesday, September 10, the South Shore Realtors Association will have a cocktail party at the poolside, and then enjoy dinner on "The Deck." Had enough? We're not through yet. On September 30, the Greater Boston YMCA will hold a 4-day conference at the Cliff until October 4.

Personal Note Dept: Daughter Gail is now living in Miami Beach, with her lovely daughter Laura, and her husband LeRoy Bailey. Roy is Director of Operations at the Fountainbleau Hotel, which was headquarters for the Republican Convention recently. If any of their friends are down that way I am sure they would love to hear from you.

My youngest son John, after graduating from Boston College 2 years ago, will enter his second year at Suffolk Law School in Boston this fall. My grandson, Aram III, son of Aram Jr. and Elizabeth, is approaching his 14-month birthday. Smart as a whip, and a real tiger! Already wants the Coffee Shop concession next summer.

Help! Help! Help! We are in need of part time waitresses both for our Dining Room and Cocktail Lounge. Please apply in person.

Too bad summer doesn't come twice a year.

When my younger brother John was old enough to help out with the hotel, we had a long-standing quote. I would set him up, as well as one or two of his friends, to do some work and leave him after saying, "let me get you started."

Aram Brazilian, Jr., 2012

NORTH SCITUATE BEACH

"News Notes"

Business is really booming at the Cliff right now. The weather for the month of July was just great and reservations are pouring in for August.

We have over 225 guests staying with us this week and all are enjoying either the ocean and sandy beach or our outdoor swimming pool. Did someone say Fun and Sun in Scituate?

Some famous guests staying with us this week are James Whitmore and Audra Lindley who starred in the recent comedy "Chic Life" at the South Shore Music Circus in Cohasset. We were especially proud that they chose to stay an extra week at the Cliff after their show had ended for rest and relaxation. Also staying at the Cliff this week was Bert Convy, Director of "Cabaret."

You remember him in "What's My Line." And the conductor of

"Cabaret" Mr. Edmund Assaly who is staying here with his lovely wife Gretta for one week.

This past Monday evening we were happy to play host to the entire cast of "Cabaret" in our Bamboo Cocktail Lounge. The stars were there, including Anna Maria Alberghetti, Sylvia Sydney, Bert Convy and a cast of 40.

The Bamboo Lounge has been the setting for all the opening night parties of the Music Circus. We received a very beautiful thank you letter from the entire cast of "Man of La Mancha" thanking the Cliff for the "pleasurable hours" spent here.

Don't forget our oceanfront Sidewalk Café for sandwiches and cocktails. Open daily at 12 noon. A magnificent view of the open Atlantic in a relaxed atmosphere!

Remember we are the only oceanfront Resort complex with sandy beach and outdoor pool from Boston to Plymouth. Join in on the fun.

Your host,
Aram Brazillian
South Shore News

Your
"HONEYMOON PACKAGE"
from the romantic

Cliff HOTEL

N. SCITUATE BEACH, MASS.

Spend Your Honeymoon at New England's Famous Cliff Hotel and Cottages

AT NORTH SCITUATE BEACH, MASS.

HONEYMOONERS have acclaimed the Cliff Hotel and the North Scituate Beach as an ideal place to spend a honeymoon. It lies in the shadow of Minot Light, which continually flashes 1-4-3 — which is the code for the words, "I Love You".

Many Travel Agents have endorsed the Cliff Hotel for Honeymoons. Mr. Rudolph Pell Ellis, who has made a complete study of places suitable for honeymoons, has given his unqualified endorsement of our place. The Saturday Evening Post, in the issue of June 23, 1951, published an article about him entitled, "Honeymoons are his Business".

A honeymoon is probably the most important vacation you will ever spend in your life. It should be perfect. It should provide a beautiful room and a private bath. It should feature a variety of activities especially suited to honeymooners.

Let us list what we have to offer you on your honeymoon.

1. A beautiful room with a private bath and delicious meals.
2. Breakfast in bed, if you wish it. Our cuisine is famous for its deliciously satisfying and wholesome qualities. Food fit for a King or Queen — cooked and served by a skilled staff. We are famous for our Sunday Buffets.
3. One of the best beaches in America.
4. Free transportation from North Scituate station — railroad or bus.

    Note: We are less than one hour's ride by rail or car from South Station, North Station or East Boston Airport. Take train from South Station and get off at North Scituate where the CLIFF HOTEL Station Wagon will meet you by arrangement, without charge.

5. Conveniences include telephone service in every room, room service, gift shop, newsstand, free transportation to shopping center, theatre and planned trips to historic points of interest and that all important Coffee Shop, open continuously, for late breakfast, lunch or midnight snacks.
6. Flowers and a bottle of beverage in your room upon arrival.
7. Dancing nightly to a well known orchestra in the romantic Brazilian Bamboo Cocktail Lounge or on the Open Air Deck.
8. A complimentary cruise of four hours. See our folder under the caption, "The Gateway to Cape Cod."
9. A sightseeing tour to historic points of interest.
10. A special party, with beverage etc., in honor of the brides preceding a dinner dance for the occasion.
11. A talent night with prizes.
12. A champagne night.
13. All sports. Sun, Surf and Sand on our private beach in front of the hotel with free use of chairs and umbrellas.
14. Complimentary use of bicycles.
15. A complimentary Golf lesson at the beautiful Hatherly Country Club.

    There is also available for your enjoyment:.

Archery	Ping Pong Swimming
Fishing	Charming Cocktail lounge.
Yachting	Shuffleboard

Golf, tennis and horse back riding — at a moderate additional charge.

For your perfect honeymoon, we are happy to offer all the above listed attractions at one all inclusive modified American Plan (Breakfast and Dinner) weekly rate of 75.00 per person.

IN REMEMBRANCE
GAIL BRAZILIAN BAILEY
1937-1976

GAIL BRAZILIAN BAILEY

Just five years old when her parents bought the Cliff Hotel, Gail grew up to be a bright, beautiful young woman. With her natural charm and gracious manner, she was a perfect partner for her mother, Elsie, helping with many of the hotel's social activities during the busy summer months.

After college, she married LeRoy Bailey, who also was in the hotel business; they had a daughter, Laura. Visits from Gail's family were welcome events, often included in Aram, Sr.'s news columns.

Above, a smiling Gail Brazilian, just selected queen, is presented with red roses by Patricia Mayglothling, President of the women's Freshman Class Council, at the Cornell freshman dance.
(Excerpt and photo from Aram Brazilian Sr.'s autobiography)

Miss Gail Brazilian, daughter of Mr. and Mrs. Aram Brazilian of North Scituate, recently graduated from Cornell University's college of Hotel Administration with a B.S. degree. She graduated from Scituate High School in 1955. At Cornell she was a member and the rushing chairman of the Kappa Kappa Gamma sorority. This summer Miss Brazilian will assist her father, owner of the Cliff Hotel, North Scituate. In the fall she will work in New York City.

Gail, Aram, Jr. and Aram, Sr. welcomed Miss Massachusetts to the Cliff Hotel.

GAIL BRAZILIAN BAILEY

Gail Brazilian Bailey passed away in 1976 at the age of 39, after a courageous battle with multiple sclerosis. She left a legacy of love and accomplishment - and many happy memories.

My daughter Gail, during her illness, occupied our house with her daughter Laura and, at times, with her husband. Her daughter slept in the same room with her mother until she was old enough to need her private room.

I converted the garage into a cozy studio bedroom, where she entertained her girl friends and studied in peaceful privacy. Gail continued to live in our house with her daughter and a maid until her death on May 5, 1976.

After my daughter's death, Laura went to live with her father. I converted her studio room into a much-needed private office where I do my paintings, violin practice, writing and office work.

(Excerpt and photo from Aram, Sr.'s autobiography)

The Miami News

(Miami, Fla.) **Gail Brazilian Bailey**, a victim of multiple sclerosis, once wrote: "there's very little I can't do...I would be thrilled to death just to stand up. Just to stand up and remember how tall I was." Mrs. Bailey never stood up again. Recently, she died of the illness that struck her at the age of 28. She was 39 years old.

A Miami resident since 1951, Mrs. Bailey graduated from Cornell University with a degree in hotel administration, and worked in that business for five years before becoming disabled. She was a member of Kappa Kappa Gamma Alumni Assn. in Miami.

She leaves her husband LeRoy, and daughter Laura, 13, her parents, Mr. and Mrs. Aram Brazilian, and two brothers, Aram Jr. and John. There will be no services. She had said earlier: "I don't want a big fuss made over me."

She wrote about the problems of raising her daughter while confined to a wheelchair in a story in the Miami News lifestyle section two years ago.

"You take each day as it comes," Mrs. Bailey wrote. "You don't look back too far. You don't worry about tomorrow. I do worry about raising my daughter. And I don't ever want to feel that just because I have MS, I can't raise her to handle her lifestyle when she's older."

She also wrote about the attitudes of those in good health to those who are handicapped:

"I had one lady push her cart into me in the supermarket six times without saying 'I'm sorry!' That's the saddest part about being disabled. People just don't see you."

She wrote about her feeling when she thought she would survive the disease:
"When I found out I wasn't dying and I knew I could raise my daughter, whether it was from a bed or a wheelchair, I was fine. I was ready to face anything. That's what I did."

THE CLIFF HOTEL AND COTTAGES are delightfully situated directly on the ocean front at North Scituate Beach, midway between Boston and Plymouth, on one of the most beautiful and interesting drives along the entire New England Coast.

Our Private Beach is the safest and finest for bathing on Massachusetts Bay. It is the ideal place for that much needed exhilarting dip in the surf or the health giving sun bath.

The accommodations at The Cliff Hotel and Cottages are modern and offer every comfort and convenience for its guests. Rooms are available in any combination desired; from single with private bath to large suites or entire cottages for families and groups. All rooms in the hotel are with bath and telephone. All public rooms are heated. Modern sprinkler system throughout, fire escape and fireproof, for your safety.

The Dining Room has won for The Cliff Hotel an enviable reputation for over twenty-five years. Only strictly fresh fruits, vegetables and seafoods are used in the preparation of the appetizing menus. Much of our produce is raised on nearby dairy and produce farms. An abundance of seafoods directly from the ocean are always available, especially Scituate famous chicken lobsters.

The Bungalows

48

Sale of the Cliff Hotel

In 1970 I decided to sell the Cliff Hotel after 28 years of operation. I wanted to devote my time to practice law. I advertised the sale of the hotel in the Boston Globe. Two young men approached me as interested buyers. On November 4, 1971 James E. Claypool and James B. Conant, both from the neighboring town of Hingham signed a purchase and sale agreement and I transferred ownership of the Cliff Hotel on December 2, 1971.

On May 23, 1974 an uncontrollable fire destroyed the five-story Cliff Hotel and adjoining three story ocean front cottage. Fire fighters from four surrounding towns had fought the blaze but could not save the Hotel nor the ocean front cottage. Aram and John both stood there watching their boyhood home engulfed and vanish in flames.

Elsie and I were 1500 miles away in our retirement home in beautiful Surfside, Florida. We began to reminisce about our 29 years of bad days and good days spent in that 75-year-old New England resort hotel. We began naming prominent public personalities who had slept under its roof. including five Governors, David I. Walsh, Michael Curley, Maurice Tobin, Charles Hurley and Paul Dever, many of whom I had supported and enjoyed their friendship.

We housed and entertained stars like Zsa Zsa Gabor and Maurice Chevalier and prominent Armenians like Alex Manoogian, Harry Adjemian and David Shakarian. Without exaggeration every insurance company and bank in greater Boston held their annual outings and clam bakes at the Cliff Hotel. Many Class Reunions of Harvard and other colleges and high schools were held there.

We were stunned and in shock from the news of the fire in "our Cliff Hotel".

Mr. and Mrs. Aram Brazilian Jr., Aram, Sr., Maurice Chevalier, Elsie and John Brazilian. (Excerpt and photo from Aram, Sr.'s autobiography)

GROWING UP AT THE CLIFF

My youngest memories were of being invisible in a living, breathing 24-hour event, which was the Cliff Hotel. I had mostly free run without very much supervision - in short, I was invisible - perfect for a kid of six or seven. Recognizing my tendency to run loose, my Dad hired an administrative assistant, Mary Tonry, who ended up half raising me in the summers. She was a wonderful, proper and stately lady who worked as his assistant from about the time I was seven until I was about 14 - by then I was beyond any hope of control, a fact which she accepted with humor and grace.

She introduced me to Durgin Park, Joseph's, and other restaurants and museums in Boston that she felt were necessary for any young person's upbringing. As well, there were always games of "Authors," and subtle suggestions that "then" and "than" had different uses. She had spent many early years in Franconia Notch, skiing, back when wooden skis were the norm. All in all, a terrific lady, and we maintained a friendship until her death when I was in college.

I remember great excursions to the Glades, past Minot and Sides Lobster pound (Sides Lobster pound was a great family business located at the edge of Minot; the house was adjacent to the beach; sea water was piped up to the retail lobster pound, where lobsters pulled from their own traps located just off shore in the cold, rocky waters provided lobsters for the locals, including many for the Cliff. Sadly, Mr. Sides was lost in a boating accident while out lobstering. For a time, his son, Wendell, took over the business. I think Wendell eventually became a marine biologist working out of Woods Hole, which seemed a fitting transition for his earlier life as the son of an authentic lobsterman. But my memories of hanging out in the lobster pound at Sides' recall a bygone era in Scituate.) The Glades had terrific rocks for diving and swimming and two WW II submarine towers. Of course admittance to the private area was restricted, but we went anyway.

From an early age I can remember my parents, in the off season, auditioning groups in the living room of our house to play in the Bamboo Room, as it was often called. Pre- rock and roll, the groups played swing music from the 40s and 50s. There were usually three to four pieces -piano, trumpet (muted) and drums. The key to any of those bands being hired was how they performed the classic, "Brazil."

Once the 60s hit, the music changed, and the auditions were carried out by my brother and then by me, along with some of my friends. I think people will remember music like "Chicago" played by the Harvard/MIT group "Pavement Narrows" (they had stolen a large yellow road sign of that wording and adopted it as their band name) who played the complete "albums" of Sgt. Pepper (Beatles) and also Fresh Cream (Cream). They were very talented and hugely popular along with another group, The Cliff Side Five.

There was also a period of time when we had jazz groups play - Mamie Lee and The Swingmen was a really talented group. They played when I was about 17 or 18.

GROWING UP AT THE CLIFF

In the winter, after the season, some of the musicians played in an after-hours club in Roxbury - it was like a speakeasy - you knocked at the door and you were checked out by the gate keeper. It was great having the door slammed in my face, then waiting around for their break and then going back in with the musicians whom I had befriended the previous summer when they played at the Cliff.

One of the best memories I have of operations at the Cliff is of the clambakes we held for insurance companies and other large companies and colleges – sometimes for as many as 400-600 persons. In those days, Smith Caterers, another family business, put on the clambakes. They would dig a large pit, line it with rocks, light a fire until the rocks were red hot, then place layers of seaweed taken from the rocks offshore, along with chicken, steamers, corn, potatoes and lobster and final cover it with a canvas tarp, letting all the layers cook in the seaweed. It was such fun to be part of all that activity - and the Hotel was a perfect setting for these groups - swimming and cocktails finished off the clambake. My friends and I would always watch the production with fascination (eating the whole time!) while chatting with the Smith family who catered the events.

No remembrance would be complete without mentioning a few of the great "regulars" over the years. Many will remember Joe Ford and Jimmy "Moon" Mullen. Joe was a great big bear of a man - perhaps gruff until you got to know him - solid as a rock and a great guy. He and Jimmy Mullen were beach and Bamboo Lounge regulars. Jimmy was a Clerk at Charlestown District Court. On warm summer days, he was at his post on the beach by 10:00 a.m., beach chair close to the water, working on his enviable suntan. He had a way of blasting through the court's business and making his escape on sunny summer days. Both he and Joe Ford would retire from the beach in the afternoons and join others for a cold beer - with ice cubes - on the patio or in the bar. These guys were fixtures, and terrific guys whom I will always remember.

Some of my friends who grew up with me at the hotel are still with us. Bill Hunter was the life guard at the pool and became a great friend; he's now a lawyer on Nantucket. We are still close friends, I'm godfather to his daughter Mei Mei, and we often have some great laughs trading stories about the Cliff days. His punishment and reward for being one of my friends was that any job assigned to me meant he was "in."

One friend who can't go unmentioned is Wayne Newcomb. Wayne came from a family that had lived in Scituate for many years. He was the first kid I marveled at my first day of kindergarten - he could kick one of those round red balls to the moon - straight up. We became fast friends, playing farm league and little league baseball together, and then football and baseball through high school. He was an All-Scholastic hockey player and all-around athlete.

Wayne basically lived at my house in the summers and was also one of my friends who learned the hotel biz from the ground up. We all used to haul the hotel's laundry up three stories with a pulley system off the back of the hotel, trading places as to which one pulled the crates in from the rope while looking down 60 feet at a landing spot if a misstep occurred. There was a period of time when the hotel offered to meet guests at Logan Airport and take them back at the end of their stay. Wayne and I were part of the bell hop crew who did the driving, sometimes five trips a day. It was madness.

GROWING UP AT THE CLIFF

Wayne enlisted in the Marines in the late 60s during the Vietnam conflict. He won the Leatherneck Dress Blue Award as the outstanding recruit at Parris Island and was deployed to Quang Nam as a Marine Recon. Wayne was killed in action during the Tet Offensive in February 1968. I was in my first year of law school when my good friend John Hayes called to tell me of the announcement in church. I always had thought of Wayne as being the luckiest guy I knew - it seemed impossible that he would be one of the war's casualties. He is missed to this day. My friends still talk about his "exploits." He was a major part of the Cliff and a larger than life personality in the best sense. Many in Scituate will remember him; guests and former workers at the Cliff certainly do.

The college kids who came each summer were also one of the best parts of growing up at the Cliff. A new crop of waiters, bell hops, bartenders, waitresses and chambermaids came from colleges all over the US, getting a summer off at the shore, learning how to work a hotel, and, I'm certain, having the best summers of their young lives. Needless to say, many new friends were made each year.

For my part, I started out washing dishes, pots and glasses, working in the kitchen, and "graduated" up to flipping burgers, bell hopping, and bussing and waiting tables. In the last years, I was in charge of training the wait staff each summer - none had prior experience - and then running the dining room.

In the off season there was plenty of time to paint, weed the gardens and carry furniture. My brother, Aram, was instrumental in supervising me and my friends - my "crew" - in our late teens and early 20s. He would yank us out of bed and drag us to the paint room or the trash/garbage room or other chamber of horrors. Once there, he would get the paint cans, brushes and rollers together - or, in the case of our all time favorite, the washing of the garbage room located under the hotel, the ammonia, buckets and scrub brushes - and then he would always say "OK, let me get you started."

My friends and I would look at each other knowingly. We were now indentured and he would be free to terrorize other employees - in those days called "The Help." I think he never called us that, and for good reason. In fairness to Aram, he did do his time painting and working very hard running the   hotel along with our parents. He was an innovator, making suggestions and improvements all the time - but still, it must have been a treat for him to have a younger brother and friends to torture with the innumerable tasks always available in a hotel like the Cliff.

We lived in the house next to the hotel. My bedroom faced the whole expanse of the structure. I can remember being a kid going to bed at night and having this living structure across the way - the sounds of people going in and out, guests, bar patrons, the cars coming into the Cliff and going down to the parking lot. I could heard the band playing or the sounds from the juke box - Tony Bennett's "I Left My Heart in San Francisco" seemed to be the favorite for so many of my younger years.

It was a great feeling knowing I could drift off to sleep with the sounds of the Cliff assuring me that I was where I was supposed to be. The hotel was filled to capacity and the lounge was bustling - no better place to be.

JOHN BRAZILIAN, 2012

Activities galore, indoor as well as outdoor. Dancing nightly in the romantic Brazilian Bamboo Cocktail Lounge or on the Open-air Deck. Bingo, cards, Community singing, Movie, Talent night with prizes, Rumba Contest, Theatre night with free transportation to the famous South Shore Players' Summer Theatre at Cohasset. *Outdoors*, Sun and Surf, the finest private Sandy Beach, at your front door. Picturesque walks on our beach promenade or verdant back woods. Golf and Tennis in the exclusive Hatherly Country Club, only five minutes' walk from the hotel, where the guests of the hotel are accorded membership privileges. Deep Sea Fishing, Cycling, Ping Pong, Croquet, Horse Shoes, Archery and Yachting.

Buffet

Cuisine: Cliff Hotel Cuisine is famous for its deliciously satisfying and wholesome qualities. Food fit for a King— cooked and served by a skilled staff. We are famous for our Sunday Buffets.

Bamboo Cocktail Lounge

Picture of Pleasure...Surf and Pool

The Crystal Clear Waters of our Swimming Pool — equipped with the most sanitary filtration system — invite you to hours of Aquatic Pleasures. Enjoy a refreshing dip here or in the ocean surf...or laze in comfort on our poolside chaises. The festive set gathers round the pool for Splash Parties...Wienie Roasts...and so much more in the way of Sun-Time Fun!

DIRECTIONS FROM NEW YORK
ONLY 250 MILES
TAKE MERRITT PARKWAY TO 15, 15 TO 20, 20 TO MASS. TURNPIKE, MASS. TURNPIKE TO 128 SOUTH, 128 SOUTH TO 3A, 3A TO NORTH SCITUATE BEACH.

Ideally Located

Less than an hour's ride by bus or car from South Station, North Station or Logan International Airport. The Cliff Hotel Station Wagon will meet you, by arrangements, without charge, at North Scituate Bus stop.

For Reservations and more information write to the Management of the Cliff Hotel, North Scituate Beach, Minot P.O. Mass., or Telephone Collect LINDEN 5-0350

The romantic Brazilian Bamboo Cocktail Lounge:

Entertainment

Nightly dancing in the Brazilian
Bamboo Cocktail Lounge or on the
open-air Deck. Talent nights . . .
contests . . . prizes.
Theatre nights with free transportation
to the famous South Shore
Music Circus at Cohasset.

Activities & Fun

The finest private Sandy
Beach at your front door.
Picturesque walks on
the beach promenade.
Golf, Deep Sea Fishing,
Horsebackriding, Tennis
nearby. Cycling, Ping Pong,
Croquet, Horse Shoes,
Badminton, Shuffleboard,
Volleyball and Archery
on the Hotel grounds.

Cliff
HOTEL and COTTAGES

A Place for Stars to Unwind
by Paul J. Reale, 1970

Next to glowing reviews, the stars of the South Shore Music Circus in Cohasset want a chance to quietly unwind a while, away from the whirligig of work, and to just be themselves with perhaps a little time for the pleasures we ordinary folks demand of summer.

Many of the headliners lodge at the Cliff Hotel in North Scituate, an immense shingled spread of 100 rooms plus cottages overlooking the beach, Minot's Light, and the sea, dating back to about 1895.

CLIFF HOTEL, NORTH SCITUATE, MASSACHUSETTS

And while Aram Brazilian and his wife Elsie, the owners-operators for 29 years, have no say as to how the critics rule, they do succeed well in satisfying the celebrities' desire for the back home comforts, including privacy, with opportunity to also sample some of South Shore style living after the rehearsals, press conferences, television-radio guest shots, and the show.

The performers are not ungrateful, for they return to the hotel when they can, bringing along family members, if possible, and greeting the proprietors often by their first names, with a siege of busses and embracing, in the manner of long-lost kin. It's an arrangement that provides the Brazilians with a view of the stars that is commonly denied theatre audiences.

"What the theater people like and what I think all the other guests like is the same thing," says Mrs. Brazilian, a slender handsomely dark and ebullient woman with a warm and easy smile. "We make everybody feel that this is a home and we are all part of the same family, anxious for everyone to be comfortable and happy."

John Carradine sort of started off on the wrong foot happiness-wise some years back and cut his comfort quotient considerably when, arriving for an engagement in Cohasset, he pulled his auto up beside the hotel one night to begin residency and neglected to set the brakes, causing the car to roll down an incline and crash into the vehicle of another guest.

But, by and large, the prevailing atmosphere at the hotel is one of serene and folksy informality, the sunny mood established by the Brazilians, who are of Armenian descent, and nurtured especially by the outgoing Mrs. Brazilian.

In addition to being the proprietress, she is a grandmother with an incorrigible fondness for all children, so that when she isn't handling business at the main desk or the

switchboard and phone reservations, or schooling the staff, or running buckets of ice, she is fussing unabashedly in the lobby over her two grandchildren, Mara and Aram III, or the youngsters of the guests, or recruiting her daughter-in-law Elizabeth, wife of Aram Jr., the general manager, for a dash upstairs to do some baby-sitting, or to help burp an infant or two and change some diapers.

"If I did not have my wife," admits Mr. Brazilian, the behind-the-scenes part of the resort operation, "I would have to add four more people to the staff."

Mrs. Brazilian often remembers the star's kids easier than she does the stars.

"Edie Adams was here this summer with three young daughters and a little son ... and, I tell you, the children were absolutely beautiful," raves Mrs. Brazilian. "That boy Joshua is the most delightful, most intelligent and best-mannered child you ever saw."

Barry Nelson and Ray Walston remained somewhat aloof during their stay as did Imogene Coca, who was unwilling even to sign autographs for guests.

However, generally speaking the actors delight in the homey pace of the hotel and contribute to it.

Maurice Chevalier, playing here eight years ago, strolled into the hotel one day and heard Aram III, weeks old at the time, screaming wildly at the main desk, while his mother, Elizabeth, and Mrs. Brazilian tried to quiet him without success. Rather than flee the howling, Chevalier stepped forward and, excusing his intrusion, lowered his famous head and crooned softly in French to the child until the tot was silent.

Betsy Palmer, performing in "Hello, Dolly!" last week, also was easy on the hotel's image. "Hi, Elsie!" she'd yell out loudly with a big smile as she breezed in after a matinee, and just as blithely she'd bounce forth in the morning for a swim in the ocean, and then seize a few minutes for some "girl talk" with Mrs. Brazilian.

⭐ *A Place for Stars to Unwind, continued*

The Music Circus administration was worried about what might happen when the tempestuous Zsa Zsa Gabor, here a few years ago for "Blithe Spirit," took up accommodations with her entourage and diminutive dog, and an advanced detail warned the Brazilians there could be problems.

However, Zsa Zsa swept in for her two-week stay and once some changes in the furnishings of her suite were made to better suit her fancy, and she was assured of a daily supply of yogurt and baskets of fresh fruit, she easily succumbed to the simple life and enjoyed herself completely.

"How do I look, dahling?" she used to call from the landing above the lobby when, dressed and dazzling and ready to hop into a chauffeured limousine to the theater, she'd appear for Mrs. Brazilian's inspection and approval.

Sid Caesar and his brother, a rotund and resolutely unsmiling gentleman, preferred not to dine before a performance and so they ordered dinners to be served after the show, about one o'clock in the morning.

Rather than risk the wrath of the chef by asking him to work after regular hours, Aram Jr. and his brother John stayed up themselves, preparing the Caesars' meals which, in truth were sumptuous feasts of both lobsters and steaks, with enormous quantities of salad. But the Caesars appreciated the Brazilians for their understanding and for their willingness to move a refrigerator into the bedroom so that cold drinks would always be easily accessible.

A hectic schedule makes it virtually impossible for the stars to stray too far from the hotel grounds and theater and, consequently, attractions such as Plymouth and Plimoth Plantation are necessarily ruled out. "They just don't have that much free time," Mrs. Brazilian sympathizes, "and yet, you know, this is still their vacation, and they've got to have some fun."

So the Brazilians enjoyed as much as anybody the nights Jo Anne Whorley, the exuberant *Laugh-In* TV star, here for "Luv" two years ago, used to "dance up a storm" before the hotel's orchestra and guests; the morning Chita Rivera ("Sweet Charity") was visited by a Franklin Park Zoo friend accompanied by a chimpanzee in diapers; and how Elaine Stritch ("Mame") who, while not a hotel guest, stopped by smoking cigars because she was trying to quit cigarettes.

They recall Molly Picon ("Milk and Honey") as a "living doll" who used to set aside a part of each day to stroll hand in hand along the beach with her husband.

Tom Poston (Edie Adams' co-star in "Plaza Suite") and his wife Kay were honeymooners when they first came to the Cliff Hotel three years ago, and now they and the Brazilians are close friends. Aram Jr. helped Tom relax from his stage chores by taking him out golfing, and Elizabeth had Kay over for lunch.

The bartenders once invited Dan Dailey ("The Odd Couple") out fishing and he enjoyed it, even though the deck chair on which he tried to sit collapsed, and the boat engine conked out, necessitating a call to the Coast Guard for help.

It seems that everybody pitches in to help the stars feel right at home. ★ ★ ★

On opening night(s), we entertained the entire cast and Music Circus officials (with) an elaborate midnight buffet, including champagne, in our Brazilian Bamboo Lounge.

Housing the stars in the Cliff Hotel created a lot of excitement and interest amongst our guests and employees. I must confess the housing of Zsa Zsa Gabor for two weeks created more excitement than any other star, except the two week stay of Maurice Chevalier, with whom we felt a close friendship.

I contrived (the) idea of a placing a sign bearing the name of the star on top of the door of the room (they had occupied) – you would be surprised how popular the idea got. We used to get reservations from guests requesting 'the room occupied by so and so star."

(Excerpt from Aram, Sr.'s autobiography

Cliff Notes, August 13, 1970

Famous guests staying at the Cliff Hotel, North Scituate Beach for the past two weeks are James Whitmore and Audra Lindley. Miss Lindley and Mr. Whitmore, who recently starred in "The Chic Life" at the South Shore Music Circus, stayed an extra week for rest and relaxation.

By the time the South Shore Music Circus was opened in 1951, its 'parent' organization had established a two-decade tradition of bringing major theatrical productions and performers to Cohasset.

In 1932, Raymond Moore, founder of the Cape Playhouse summer theater in Dennis chose Cohasset's historic town hall as a second performance venue, which brought stars like Humphrey Bogart, Josephine Hull and Van Heflin to the South Shore.

The South Shore Players began the following year, formed by new manager Alexander Dean, and live performances continued in Cohasset featuring foremost writers and actors, including Edward Everett Horton, Arthur Treacher, Sylvia Sydney, Thornton Wilder and Sinclair Lewis.

By 1949, the Players were outgrowing the town hall, and a group of residents set about to create a performing arts center that could serve neighboring communities as well, for the benefit of the South Shore communities.

"It was around this time that the first tent theatres began operating on the east coast, the first in New Jersey, the second in Florida. When famed English actress Gertrude Lawrence viewed the Florida tent theatre, she convinced her husband, Richard Aldrich, that New England would be a great location for this summer theatre concept. (They) first approached the South Shore Players with the idea for a tent theatre for musicals, but at the time it didn't coincide with the theatre they envisioned," according to notes on the South Shore Music Circus website, which are the source for this information. "There was, however, interest in Hyannis, so in 1950, the Cape Cod Music Circus (now the Cape Cod Melody Tent) became the third musical tent to open in the US."

"On December 10, 1950, the South Shore Playhouse Associates, Inc. announced that they would begin presenting operettas and musical shows on the "horse grounds" of the Bancroft Estate in Cohasset ... known as the South Shore Music Circus, Inc. ... (it) would retain the services of the eminent Broadway producer and director of the Cape Playhouse and the Hyannis Music Circus, Richard Aldrich.

"The South Shore Music Circus became musical tent number four ... The landscape of the Bancroft Estate changed to accommodate the tent ... Vestiges of the "horse grounds" still exist today – the grassy area in the parking lot was once part of the Bancroft's horse ring and is maintained as a tribute to the theatre's origin.

"On June 25, 1951, the South Shore Music Circus presented its first show – a performance of Show Boat – boasting a cast of sixty. Interest in this new theatre was so great that the first four performances of that season sold out in advance and the remaining three had near capacity crowds." Tickets for that first season sold for $1.20 to $3.60 for the evening performances and $1.20 to $3.00 for the matinee on Thursday."

CELEBRITY GUESTS

MUSIC CIRCUS STARS

The world-renowned actors who stayed at The Cliff Hotel brought glamour and recognition not only to the hotel, but to Scituate, as well.

EDIE ADAMS (1927-2008)

Edie Adams had a remarkably varied career in show business performing on stage, in nightclubs and on the large and small screens – yet she became best known, for her sensual delivery pitching cigars in taunting 60s ads and commercials with her sultry line, "Why don't you pick one up and smoke it sometime?"

A classically trained singer who graduated from Juilliard, she won the Miss U.S. Television beauty pageant in 1950 after singing a coloratura version of "Love Is Where You Find It" in the talent competition. The prize was an appearance in Minneapolis onstage with Milton Berle, which led to a spot on his television show, which in turn led to her being featured on television with the cigar-smoking comedian Ernie Kovacs, who would become her husband.

She made her Broadway debut in 1953 playing Rosalind Russell's sister in the Leonard Bernstein musical Wonderful Town. She won a Tony in 1956 for her second Broadway role as *Daisy Mae in Li'l Abner.*

In the 1960s she appeared in a number of supporting roles in battle-of-the-sexes films including *The Apartment* with Jack Lemmon and Shirley MacLaine and *Lover Come Back*, with Doris Day and Rock Hudson. She also was part of the enormous ensemble cast that included Sid Caesar, Jonathan Winters, Spencer Tracy, Phil Silvers, Mickey Rooney and Ethel Merman in Stanley Kramer's *It's A Mad, Mad, Mad World.*

ANNA MARIA ALBERGHETTI (b. 1924)

Born in Pesaro, Italy, the daughter of a concertmaster father and pianist mother, Anna was performing with symphony orchestras by the age of six. When her family moved to the United States during World War II, 14-year old Anna enthralled American audiences with her pure operatic tones during a Carnegie Hall debut.

The family settled permanently in the States, and Anna performed with many symphony orchestras during her teens. In 1950, recognizing star potential in the lovely young woman with the angelic voice, Paramount Pictures cast her in Gian Carlo Menotti's chamber opera, *The Medium.*

After her magical debut, Paramount wasted no time finding more mainstream film roles for her. She had an extended operatic solo in the Bing Crosby/Jane Wyman comedy *Here Comes the Groom*. In *The Stars Are Singing*, with Rosemary Clooney, Anna again captivated audiences with her touching renditions of *My Kind of Day* and *My Heart Is Home*.

Then, inexplicably, her vocal talents were overlooked as she was cast in several rugged adventure films and light comedies. After appearing in Jerry Lewis's gender-bending musical farce, *Cinderfella,* when Lewis kept all the songs for himself, Anna decided to pursue a career on Broadway.

Following a role in the operetta "Rose Marie" in 1960, she played Lili in the musical *Carnival*, for which she won a Tony. Throughout the 60s, she enjoyed success in musical ingénue roles, including the title role in *Fanny*, Maria in *West Side Story*, and Luisa in *The Fantasticks*.

Ed Sullivan introduced Anna to TV audiences, and invited her back to the show 53 times. She won non-singing roles on a number of TV shows, and had a successful recording career with Capitol, Columbia, Mercury and MGM Records.

After taking time off to raise two daughters, Anna returned to television in the 70s as the spokeswoman for "Good Seasons" salad dressing.

THEODORE BIKEL (b. 1924)

Born in Vienna, Austria, Bikel studied at London's Royal Academy of Dramatic Art, graduating with honors. Next stop - London's West End, the mecca of all English actors, where he played Mitch in *Streetcar Named Desire*, starring Vivien Leigh.

While appearing in the West End play *Dear Charles* in 1954, he received an invitation to appear on Broadway in *Tonight in Samarkand*. He's appeared on Broadway in more than 40 productions, including the 1959 world premiere of *The Sound of Music,* in which he created the role of Captain von Trapp and *My Fair Lady*. Since his first appearance as Tevye in the musical *Fiddler on the Roof* in 1967, Bikel has performed the role more often than any other actor (more than 2,000 times to date).

His 36 movie performances include *The African Queen, The Enemy Below* and *The Russians Are Coming, the Russians Are Coming* – and Frank Zappa's 1971 film *200 Motels*. Among his TV credits are guest appearances on Rod Serling's *The Twilight Zone, Wagon Train, Columbo, Gunsmoke, Dynasty, All in The Family, Law & Order* and *Star Trek: The Next Generation*.

A gifted folk singer, Bikel was a co-founder of the Newport Folk Festival (together with Pete Seeger and George Wein) in 1959. He was president of Actors' Equity in the late 1970s and early 1980s, and was appointed to serve on the National Council on the Arts by President Jimmy Carter in 1977.

JOHN CARRADINE (1906-1988)

Considered one of Hollywood's most prolific character actors, Carradine worked as a painter and sculptor before making his acting debut in a production of *Camille* in New Orleans in 1925.

Arriving in Los Angeles in 1927, he worked in local theatre. When he applied to be a scenic designer for Cecil B. DeMille, the legendary director rejected his designs but gave him voice work in several films. Nearly three decades later, he acted in a DeMille production, portraying Aaron in *The Ten Commandments*.

His on-screen debut was in *Tol'able David* (1930). By 1936, he'd become a member of director John Ford's stock company, appearing first in *The Prisoner of Shark Island*. Carradine would make 11 pictures with Ford, including his first important role, as Preacher Casey in *The Grapes of Wrath* (1940), which starred Henry Fonda and *The Man Who Shot Liberty Valance* (1962) and *Stagecoach* (1939), both with John Wayne. In a career that spanned 50 years, Carradine appeared in more than 300 films, often playing eccentric, insane or diabolical characters, especially in the horror genre, where he had become identified as a 'star' by the mid-1940s. His more contemporary movie credits include *The Ice Pirates* (1984) and *Peggy Sue Got Married* (1986). He also was the voice of the Great Owl in 1982's *The Secret of NIMH*.

Carradine won a Daytime Emmy Award in 1985 for his performance in the Young People's Special *Umbrella Jack*, one of his more than 100 TV roles.

Married four times, Carradine fathered four children, including actors David and Keith Carradine; actress Martha Plimpton is his granddaughter. John Carradine died at the age of 82, just hours after climbing the 328 steep steps of the Duomo, Milan, Italy's gothic cathedral.

MAURICE CHEVALIER (1888-1972)

Born in Paris, Chevalier worked as a farmer, circus acrobat, cabaret singer and, starting in 1908, as a comical actor in French films, including Chaplin's *A Woman of Paris*. In 1909, his first major engagement as a mimic and a singer in *l'Alcazar* received critical acclaim from French theatre critics. His performance in the operetta *Dédé* earned praise as well, and in 1922 George Gershwin and Irving Berlin the play, and Chevalier, to Broadway.

He made his first American movie in 1929, *The Love Parade*, with operatic singer/actress Jeanette MacDonald. They did two more pictures after that. The film was a success and Chevalier made more successful films with directors like Ernst Lubitsch *(The Merry Widow, 1934))*.

He made *Gigi* – perhaps his most familiar role – in 1958, from which he took his signature songs, "Thank Heaven for Little Girls" and "I Remember it Well," and received a special Oscar that year.

In the early 1960s, he toured the United States, and between 1960 and 1963 made eight films, including *Can-Can* (1960) with Frank Sinatra. In 1961, he starred in the drama *Fanny* with Leslie Caron and Charles Boyer, followed by *Panic Button* with Jayne Mansfield. In 1965, at 77, he made another world tour. In 1967 he toured in Latin America, again the US, Europe and Canada. The following year, on October 1, 1968, he announced his farewell tour.

In 1970, Chevalier sang the title song for Walt Disney's The AristoCats, which was his final contribution to the film industry.

SID CAESAR (b. 1922)

As a young waiter in his parents' Yonkers, New York restaurant, Sid Caesar learned to mimic the many accents that eventually would become the basis for his successful comedic career.

But his original interest was music. At fourteen, Caesar went to the Catskills as a saxophonist with a swing band where he'd occasionally perform in sketches. After graduating from high school, he returned to the Catskills to work at the Vacationland Hotel, where he played in the band and learned to perform comedy, doing three shows a week.

In 1939, he enlisted in the United States Coast Guard, and was assigned to play in military revues and shows in Brooklyn. While performing in a service revue, *Tars and Spars*, he met Max Liebman, later the producer of his first hit television series. Caesar began his television career on Milton Berle's *Texaco Star Theater*. In early 1949, he met his future sidekick, Imogene Coca, while appearing in *The Admiral Broadway Revue*.

His appearance in the first episode of *Your Show of Shows* in February 1950 launched Caesar into instant stardom. A brilliant mix of scripted and improvised comedy, movie and television satires, Caesar's monologues, top musical guests, and large production numbers, it brought together one of the best comedy teams in television history: Caesar, Carl Reiner, Howard Morris and Imogene Coca, and a stellar team of writers, including Mel Brooks, Neil Simon, Woody Allen, and Larry Gelbart.

Shortly after the show ended in 1954, Caesar returned with *Caesar's Hour*, a variety show which ran for three years with Morris, Reiner, Bea Arthur and Nanette Fabray.

Throughout the years, Caesar remained active, making occasional television and night club appearances, and starring in several movies including *Silent Movie*, *History of the World*, *Part I*, *Airport 1975*, *Grease* and *Grease 2*.

In 1997, Caesar joined fellow TV icons Bob Hope and Milton Berle at the Primetime Emmy Awards 50th anniversary. He received the 'Pioneer Award' at the 2006 TV Land Awards.

IMOGENE COCA   (1908-2001)

Best remembered for her comedic partnership with Sid Caesar in NBC's live Saturday night program, *Your Show of Shows,* Coca did not begin her career in comedy. The daughter of a violinist/orchestra conductor and a chorus girl, Imogene started piano lessons, vocal training and dance classes at a very tender age.

She made her Broadway debut in 1925, at 17 in the chorus of *When You Smile*; for the next 30 years she could be found doing musical revues, as well as solo acts in Manhattan clubs, such as the Rainbow Room and the Silver Slipper.

Her comedic skills emerged during rehearsals for *New Faces of 1934*, and she honed them working in the Poconos with performers like Danny Kaye and Carol Channing.

In 1949, she was paired with Caesar in NBC's "*The Admiral's Broadway Revue,*" and the two found fame together on *Your Show of Shows* launched the next year. Coca won an Emmy for the program in 1951.

In the sixties and seventies, Coca starred in two single-season sitcoms (NBC's *Grindl* and *It's About Time* on CBS), and made guest appearances on Dick Cavett's talk show, *The Carol Burnett Show*, and series such as *Bewitched*, *Moonlighting* and *One Life to Live*. In 1983, at the age of 75, she made the most of her appearance as Aunt Edna in *National Lampoon's Vacation*.

She paved the way for a new generation of female comedians like Lily Tomlin, Whoopi Goldberg and Tracey Ullman, all of whom acknowledged her inspiration.

A humanitarian and animal lover, she founded the Imogene Coca Charitable Foundation which still supports the Humane Society as well as human and civil rights organizations.

JAMES CROMWELL (b. 1940)

Following acting studies at Carnegie -Mellon, James Cromwell - the son of noted film director John Cromwell and actress Kay Johnson - went into the theater, doing everything from Shakespeare to experimental plays.

Cromwell's first television performance was in a 1974 episode of *The Rockford Files*. Several weeks later, he began a recurring role as Stretch Cunningham on *All in the Family*.

In 1975, he got his first lead role on television as Bill Lewis in the short-lived *Hot l Baltimore*, and a year later he made his film debut in Neil Simon's classic detective spoof *Murder by Death*.

His supporting roles in the films *Tank* and *Revenge of the Nerds* were gaining notice. And his starring roles in *Babe* (for which he earned an Academy Award nomination), *L.A. Confidential*, and *The Green Mile*, made him more bankable in Hollywood.

His role as newspaper tycoon William Randolph Hearst in the television film *RKO 281* earned him an Emmy Award nomination for Outstanding Supporting Actor in a Television Movie. He was nominated again twice for his roles as Bishop Lionel Stewart on *ER* and President D. Wire Newman on *The West Wing*. He portrayed a U.S. President three more times - fictional President Fowler in *The Sum of All Fears*, Lyndon Johnson in the TV movie *RFK,* and George H.W. Bush in Oliver Stone's film *W*.

From 2003 to 2005, Cromwell played George Sibley in the HBO drama series *Six Feet Under* and was again nominated for an Emmy, this time in the TV series category.

In 2006, Cromwell played Prince Philip, Duke of Edinburgh in *The Queen*, and guest starred as Phillip Bauer, father of lead character Jack, in the sixth season of the Fox thriller drama series *24*.

Cromwell received the King Vidor Memorial Award from the San Luis Obispo International Film Festival in 2007 for his artistic achievements in film.

DAN DAILEY (1915-1978)

Born in New York City, Dan Dailey appeared in a minstrel show when he was very young, and worked in vaudeville before his Broadway debut in 1937 in *Babes in Arms*. Signed by MGM to make movies in 1940, he was initially cast as a Nazi in *The Mortal Storm* and a mobster in *The Get Away*, although his past career had been in musicals. The MGM folks soon realized their mistake, and his successful career in musical films was launched.

During World War II, Dailey was commissioned as an Army officer after graduation from Signal Corps Officer Candidate School at Fort Monmouth, NJ. After his discharge, he went back to Hollywood to resume that career.

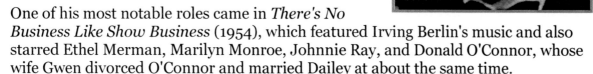

Beginning with *Mother Wore Tights* in 1947, Dailey became the frequent and favorite co-star of movie legend Betty Grable. His performance in their film *When My Baby Smiles at Me* in 1948 garnered him an Academy Award nomination for Best Actor.

In 1950, he starred in *A Ticket to Tomahawk*, often noted as one of the first screen appearances of Marilyn Monroe, in a very small part as a dance-hall girl. He portrayed baseball pitcher Dizzy Dean in a 1952 biopic, *Pride of St. Louis.*

One of his most notable roles came in *There's No Business Like Show Business* (1954), which featured Irving Berlin's music and also starred Ethel Merman, Marilyn Monroe, Johnnie Ray, and Donald O'Connor, whose wife Gwen divorced O'Connor and married Dailey at about the same time.

As the musical genre began to wane in the mid-1950s, Dailey moved on to various comedic and dramatic roles, including appearing as one of *The Four Just Men* (1959) in the Sapphire Films TV series for ITV, his own television series, *The Governor & J.J.* and the NBC Mystery Movie series *Faraday & Company.*

In the late 1960s, Dan Dailey toured as Oscar Madison in a road production of *The Odd Couple*, co-starring Elliott Reid as Felix Unger and Peter Boyle as Murray the cop.

Zsa Zsa Gabor (b. 1917)

Born in Budapest, Hungary, the middle daughter of Vilmos Gabor, a soldier, and Jolie Gabor, the heiress to a European jewelry business, Gabor and her two sisters, Eva and Magda, lived a life of luxury, which included a staff of servants, extensive vacations, and stints at expensive boarding schools.

At the age of 13, Gabor attended boarding school in Lausarine, Switzerland, where she was discovered by the famous operatic tenor Richard Tauber, who invited her to sing the soubrette in his new operetta, Der singende Traum.

She went on to study at the Vienna Acting Academy, and made her acting debut at the age of 15. That same year, Gabor married her first husband, 35-year-old Turkish government official Burhan Asaf Belge, to whom she proposed.

Gabor was crowned Miss Hungary in 1936. In 1941, with both of their marriages over, Zsa Zsa and her mother emigrated to the United States. Shortly after their arrival, Gabor met hotel magnate Conrad Hilton at an upscale club, where he reportedly offered her $20,000 to accompany him to Florida. She refused. Four months later, they married; they had a daughter, Francesca, before their divorce just five years later.

Zsa Zsa's good looks and charm landed her a film career in Hollywood. Beginning in 1952 she made her big-screen debut in *Lovely to Look At*. That year, she also had a part in *We're Not Married!* with Ginger Rogers and Fred Astaire, and a starring role in *Moulin Rouge* with José Ferrer. She later appeared with George Sanders (who became her third husband) in *Death of a Scoundrel* and had a small role in Orson Welles' classic *Touch of Evil*. Zsa Zsa made more than 40 films over the next 50 years.

Also in the 1950s Gabor made guest appearances on more than 50 television shows, including *The Life of Riley, Playhouse 90, Matinee Theatre, Burke's Law, Gilligan's Island*, and *Batman*.

Vivacious and humorous, she also was a popular guest on talk shows and celebrity game shows, where audiences seemed more interested in her personal life than her acting career. Besides her film and television appearances, she is best known for having nine husbands – and for her oft-mimicked habit of calling everyone, "dah-link."

When Zsa Zsa Gabor stayed at the hotel, her boyfriend climbed up on the roof and climbed in a window to her room … when she stayed with us, she had 3 rooms - one for her, one for her clothes, and one for her assistant and dog. We would remove all of the furniture from one room and fill it with all of her clothes.

Aram Brazilian, Jr., 2012

JULIUS LAROSA (b. 1930)

Julius La Rosa joined the United States Navy at age 17 as a radioman, singing in a Navy choir and at the officers club, La Rosa earned many fans.

A Navy buddy who knew Arthur Godfrey arranged an audition for LaRosa with the iconic radio and TV personality. Impressed, Godfrey invited La Rosa to appear on his television show, ending the spot by saying, "When Julie gets out of the Navy, he'll come back to see us."

One week after his discharge, in 1951, La Rosa was hired as a regular on both *Arthur Godfrey Time* and *Arthur Godfrey and His Friends*.

In 1952, Godfrey's bandleader Archie Bleyer, formed Cadence Records and signed La Rosa, who recorded the label's first single, *Anywhere I Wander*. The song was the first of several successful recordings and, despite Godfrey's objection, La Rosa hired a personal agent and manager.

As the singer's popularity grew and his fan mail surpassed Godfrey's, the relationship became more strained. On the October 19, 1953 morning show, after La Rosa finished singing "Manhattan," a disgruntled Godfrey fired him on the air. Ed Sullivan immediately signed the young star for his CBS Toast of the Town TV variety show.

At the same time, La Rosa's recording career was flourishing. A new song, *Eh, Cumpari,* hit #1 on the Cash Box chart and #2 on the Billboard chart, earning La Rosa an award as the best new male vocalist of 1953.

He was a guest on many TV shows, including *What's My Line?, The Merv Griffin Show,* and *Laverne and Shirley*, and had an Emmy nominated role on *Another World.*

La Rosa eventually went to work as a deejay for New York radio stations WNEW and WNSW, and performed in cabarets and small concert venues until 2008.

AUDRA LINDLEY   (1918-1997)

Audra Lindley, daughter of stage and film actor Bert Lindley, got her early start in Hollywood as a stand-in which eventually progressed to stunt work. After a while, however, she found stunt work not to her liking and went to New York in her mid-20s to take her talent to the stage.

Among her many Broadway plays were *On Golden Pond, Long Day's Journey into Night*, and *Horse Heavens.*

She began to make steady appearances on television as well, including the role of Sue Knowles on the CBS soap opera *Search for Tomorrow*, and a six-year stint as manipulative "Aunt Liz" Matthews on the NBC soap opera *Another World*. She also appeared regularly in roles as Meredith Baxter's mother in the sitcom *Bridget Loves Bernie*, and Lee Grant's best friend in *Fay.*

Lindley is, perhaps, best known for her work as the wisecracking, perpetually unfulfilled and frustrated Helen Roper on the hit sitcom *Three's Company* opposite Norman Fell as the clueless skinflint, Mr. Roper. The characters later had their own sitcom, *The Ropers*, which lasted two seasons (1979-80).

After *The Ropers* ended, Lindley continued to find interesting roles, working steadily on television and in film until her death from leukemia in 1997. On the big screen, she turned in memorable performances as Fauna, the owner of the Bear Flag Restaurant, a brothel portrayed in *Cannery Row*, starring Nick Nolte and Debra Winger, and in *Best Friends*, with Goldie Hawn and Burt Reynolds.

Her notable TV appearances included *Revenge of the Stepford Wives* and playing Phoebe Buffay's grandmother on *Friends*. A recurring role as Cybill Shepherd's mother on the CBS sitcom *Cybill* (whose mother she had played in the 1972 film *The Heartbreak Kid*) was her last.

HAL MARCH (1920-1970)

Hal March first came on the scene in 1944 as one half of the comedy duo, Sweeney & March, who had their own CBS radio program until 1948. In the early fifties, he had some uncredited movie roles and appeared on several TV shows such as *I Love Lucy* and *The Kate Smith Evening Hour*.

His big break came when he was hired to host *The $64,000 Question*, where his personality and the astronomical prize money made it the undisputed king of game shows. After three years, disaster struck when the $64,000 Question fell victim to the infamous Quiz Show Scandals.

When the showed closed, March won roles on TV programs like *The Schlitz Playhouse*, *Westinghouse Preview Theater* and *The DuPont Show of the Week*. On Broadway, he replaced Henry Fonda in *Two for the Season*, and appeared in Neil Simon's *Come Blow Your Horn*.

March appeared on *The Lucy Show* and *The Monkees*; he also appeared in and worked as the technical adviser on *A Guide for the Married Man* and made occasional guest appearances on a variety of television shows such as *Here's Hollywood*, *I've Got a Secret*, and even a guest host stint on *The Tonight Show*.

In 1969, March finally returned to game shows, hosting *It's Your Bet*, but after just 13 weeks of taping, March was diagnosed with lung cancer. He died at the age of 49 in 1970. He has two stars on the Hollywood Walk of Fame, one for his work in radio and one for his work in television.

JOAN MCINTOSH (b. 1946)

An Associate Professor at Yale, McIntosh has had an acclaimed career as an actress for over 40 years.

A co-founder of the internationally celebrated experimental theatre company, The Performance Group, she won OBIES for *Dionysus in 69*, *The Tooth of Crime*, and for Distinguished Performance in *Commune*.

Her impressive portfolio of acclaimed dramatic performances includes appearances on Broadway, and at the National Actor's Theatre, Lincoln Center Theater, and New York Shakespeare Festival New York Theatre Workshop. Her honors include a Drama League Award for Distinguished Performance, the Edinburgh Festival Herald Angel Award for Distinguished Performance, a Drama Desk Award and the 2007 Eliot Norton Award.

She is currently writing a book about her experiences with The Performance Group.

BARRY NELSON   (1917-2007)

Nelson began acting in school at the age of fifteen. After graduating from UC/Berkeley in 1941, he was signed as an MGM contract player, making his screen debut in *Shadow of the Thin Man* with William Powell and Myrna Loy. Roles in *Johnny Eager* and *A Yank on the Burma Road* followed.

Joining the Army and assigned to an entertainment unit, he made his Broadway debut in 1943, billed as Pvt. Barry Nelson in Moss Hart's wartime morale builder, *Winged Victory*, and also appeared in the 1944 film version of the play. Hart cast Nelson in his next play, *Light Up the Sky* the following year.

Over the years, he had roles in many plays including the original production of *The Moon is Blue, Cactus Flower* with Lauren Bacall, and both the stage and screen versions of *Mary, Mary*. In 1978, he was nominated for a Tony Award for Best Actor in a Musical for his role as Dan Connors in *The Act* with Liza Minnelli. He made his final Broadway appearance on Broadway in *42nd Street* (1986).

Nelson was the first actor to play James Bond on screen, in a 1954 adaptation of Ian Fleming's novel *Casino Royale* on the television anthology series *Climax!* He appeared regularly on television in the 1960s, in such diverse venues as *Alfred Hitchcock Presents, The Twilight Zone, Dr. Kildare, Murder, She Wrote*, and *Dallas*.

BETSY PALMER   (b. 1926)

Less than a week after she arrived in New York City, Palmer got her first acting job in 1951 when she joined the cast of a 15-minute daily soap opera, *Miss Susan* in Philadelphia. She was "discovered" for this role at a party in the apartment of actor Frank Sutton.

Palmer first appeared on Broadway in *The Grand Prize.* Later stage credits included *Forty Carats,* and extensive touring in the role of Nellie Forbush in *South Pacific.*

She become a familiar face on television as a regular panelist on the quiz show *I've Got a Secret* from 1958 -1967. Palmer created the role of Suz Becker on *As the World Turns* and appeared on *Knots Landing* as Valene Ewing's aunt, Virginia "Ginny" Bullock.

Palmer appeared in many movies during the 1950s, including *The Long Gray Line* with Tyrone Power and The *Queen Bee*, which starred Joan Crawford. She also played nurse Lt. Ann Girard, the lead female role in the all-star cast of the classic film *Mister Roberts* which starred Henry Fonda, Jack Lemmon, and James Cagney.

She accepted what would become her most famous role – Pamela Voorhees in *Friday the 13th* because she needed a new car. Despite her distaste for the film, she consented to a cameo appearance in *Friday the 13th Part 2*.

MOLLY PICON (1898-1992)

Born in New York City to immigrant Polish parents, Picon debuted in 1912 at the *Arch Street Theatre* in New York and became a star of the Second Avenue Yiddish stage. Later, as Yiddish theatre faded, she began to perform in English-language productions.

Picon appeared on Second Avenue in many productions including *Yankele* and *Mamale*. She also made movies in Europe, including *Yidl Mit'n Fidl*, which was the last Jewish film made in Poland before the Nazi occupation.

In 1940, Picon began a long-running radio show sponsored by Jell-O and Maxwell House Coffee, and made her English language stage debut.

Picon's first major English speaking role was in the film version of *Come Blow Your Horn* (1963), with Frank Sinatra. She also portrayed Yente the Matchmaker in the film adaptation of the Broadway hit *Fiddler on the Roof* in 1971. Her television work included the soap opera *Somerset*, *The Facts of Life*, *Gomer Pyle USMC*, and a recurring role as Mrs. Bronson in the series *Car 54, Where Are You?*

TOM POSTON (1921-2007)

Born in Columbus, Ohio, Poston's boyhood dream was to be a prizefighter. As a young man he boxed in amateur fights. Later he enrolled at Bethany College to study chemistry, dropping out to serve in the Army Air Corps in Europe in World War II.

After the war, Poston studied at the American Academy of Dramatic Art and made his Broadway debut in José Ferrer's production of *Cyrano de Bergerac*. He earned acclaim in other classic plays such as *The Barretts of Wimpole Street* and *King Lear*, but comedy beckoned.

Hosting the TV show *Entertainment* led to a recurring role on the *Steve Allen Plymouth Show* for which he won an Emmy in 1959. He appeared frequently as a television game show panelist including regular appearances on *To Tell the Truth* and *What's My Line?* In addition to his best-known television roles as George Utley on *Newhart* and Mr. Bickley on *Mork & Mindy*, he appeared on many other programs including *Murphy Brown, ER, Ellen, Will & Grace, The Simpsons* and *Coach*.

Broadway appearances included *Will Success Spoil Rock Hunter?, Mary, Mary* and the 1972 revival of *A Funny Thing Happened on the Way to the Forum*. Among his movies were *Christmas With the Kranks* and *The Princess Diaries 2*.

In 2006 Poston guest-starred on an episode of *The Suite Life of Zack & Cody*, which was his final role.

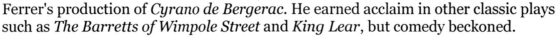

♛ I played golf with Tom Poston at Hatherly Country Club. He took his shirt off and was kicked out for refusing to put it back on. Aram Brazilian, Jr., 2012

CHITA RIVERA (b. 1933)

Rivera's mother enrolled her in the Jones-Haywood School of Ballet in 1933 when she was 11 years old. Four years later she won a scholarship to study at the prestigious George Balanchine School of American Ballet in New York City.

In 1951, Rivera accompanied a friend to the audition for the touring company of *Call Me Madam* and ended up winning the role herself. She went on to land roles in other Broadway productions such as *Guys and Dolls* and *Can-Can*. In 1957, she was cast in the role that cemented her stardom as Anita in *West Side Story*. Rivera starred in a national tour of *Can-Can* and played Nicky in the film adaptation of *Sweet Charity* with Shirley MacLaine. In 1975 she appeared as Velma Kelly in the original cast of the musical *Chicago*. She won her first Tony in 1984 for her role as Anna in the musical *The Rink*.

After a two-year hiatus to recover from severe injuries sustained in a car accident in 1986, Rivera returned to the stage. In 1993, she received a Tony Award for Best Leading Actress in a Musical for her portrayal of Aurora in the musical *Kiss of the Spider Woman*. A decade later in the 2003 revival of *Nine* as Liliane La Fleur, Rivera received her eighth career Tony Award nomination and fourth Drama Desk Award nomination. *Chita Rivera: The Dancer's Life*, a retrospective of her career opened on Broadway in 2005, and Rivera received another Tony nomination for her self-portrayal.

In the 1960s she recorded two albums, *Chita Rivera: Get Me To The Church On Time* and *And Now I Sing*. She released her third solo album, *And Now I Swing in 2008*.

In 2012, at the age of 79, Rivera will play Princess Puffer in the Broadway musical *The Mystery of Edwin Drood* starting in November as this publication goes to press.

Rivera is the first Hispanic woman to receive a Kennedy Center Honors award. She also received the Presidential Medal of Freedom in 2009.

RAY WALSTON (1914-2001)

Walston began acting with the Margo Jones Community Players in Houston, Texas, in 1938, and for almost four years he performed in a play every month. In 1943, he made his professional stage debut in Tennessee Williams' first play, *You Touch Me,* at the Cleveland Playhouse.

Walston went to New York in 1945 and found consistent work on Broadway. In 1949, he won a Clarence Dewart Award playing Mr. Kramer in Tennessee Williams' *Summer and Smoke*. In 1950, he played Luther Billis in *South Pacific* both on Broadway and in a nine-month London's Drury Lane Theatre. He appeared in another Rogers and Hammerstein production, *Me and Juliet*, as well as a musical written by Truman Capote, *House of Flowers*. In 1956 Walston won a Tony Award for Best Actor in the Musical, *Damn Yankees*, opposite Gwen Verdon.

In 1957 Walston made a film with Cary Grant and Jayne Mansfield in *Kiss Them For Me*, followed by character roles in the screen version of *Damn Yankees, South Pacific* and *The Apartment*.

But it was in the title role of TV's My Favorite Martian that America fell in love with Ray Walston. When he left the show after three seasons, he fought hard to leave that role behind, reviving his film career with several hits including *The Sting, Silver Streak* and *Fast Times at Ridgemont High*.

At the age of 77, Walston again created a fresh, unique character with Judge Henry Bone in *Picket Fences,* for which he was twice awarded the Emmy for Best Supporting Actor in a Dramatic Series.

JAMES WHITMORE (1921-2009)

Whitmore earned his BA from Yale University in 1944 before serving with the Marines in World War II. Following his discharge, he went under the G.I. bill to the American Theatre Wing.

Whitmore's 1947 Broadway debut as Tech Sergeant Evans in *Command Decision* reaped the stage acting trifecta: the Tony, Donaldson and Theatre World awards.

His first film role in the documentary-styled crime thriller *The Undercover Man* (1949) led to a role in Battleground for which he won a Golden Globe and an Oscar nomination. In the 1950s, he appeared in a number of diverse films from the gritty drama *The Asphalt Jungle* and the musical *Kiss Me Kate* to *Them!,* one of the more intelligent sci-fi dramas of the 1950s.

During that time, he also turned in memorable television performances in *The Twilight Zone, The Detectives, Ben Casey* and a host of live theater dramas as well as his own two-season series, *The Law and Mr. Jones*.

But every so often a marvelous character role would call him back to films. Notable were his white man role passing for black in *Black Like Me*, his weary veteran cop in *Madigan*, and his brash, authoritative simian in the classic sci-fi *Planet of the Apes*.

Whitmore and his second wife actress Audra Lindley forged a strong acting partnership, earning critical success for their appearances together in such plays as *The Magnificent Yankee, On Golden Pond, The Visit, Foxfire* and *Love Letters*.

In the 1970s Whitmore turned to one-man stage performances portraying such legends as Will Rogers, Harry Truman and Theodore Roosevelt, all of which were preserved on film and TV in the form of *Will Rogers' USA* (TV); *Give 'em Hell, Harry!*, which earned him his second Oscar nomination; and *Bully: An Adventure with Teddy Roosevelt*.

In his 70s Whitmore turned in strong performances with his touching role as an aged, ill-fated prison parolee in *The Shawshank Redemption* in 1994 and winning an Emmy for a recurring part on *The Practice*.

JOANNE WORLEY (b. 1937)

The third of five children, Worley learned early on to separate herself from the crowd with her distinctively loud voice. Crowned 'school comedienne' at her Indiana high school, she attended Midwestern State University on a two-year drama scholarship, then went to Los Angeles City College and trained at the Pasadena Playhouse. She made her professional debut in a production of *Wonderful Town,* and garnered some attention in the L.A. musical revue *Billy Barnes' People,* a show that took her all the way to Broadway.

In 1966, while showcasing her nightclub act in Greenwich Village, she was 'discovered' by talk-show host Merv Griffin who had her on his show approximately 200 times. Producer George Schlatter saw her on the show and hired her for the ensemble of *Rowan & Martin's Laugh-In,* where her manic energy and faux operatic tones made her a TV star.

Leaving *Laugh-In* for greener pastures, Worley made onscreen guest appearances on several TV shows and was a familiar face on the talk show, variety show and game show circuits. But she never found another TV vehicle for her brand of zaniness.

She found her niche in musical theater, touring with dozens of productions including *Gypsy, Mame, Annie Get Your Gun and Nunsense.* Her non-singing theater resume includes *Same Time, Next Year, Lovers and Other Strangers, Steel Magnolias,* and the female version of *The Odd Couple.*

Worley has served on the Board of Directors for Actors and Others for Animals and also has been seen whipping up specialties on several Food Network programs.

GOOD SPORTS

The Boston Bruins celebrated their 1970-1971 and 1972-73 Stanley Cup Championships at the Cliff Hotel. Aram, Jr. claims to have a photo of Bobby Orr in a tub of champagne.

We do, however, have these great shots of Aram, Jr., his wife Elizabeth and Aram, Sr. with Bobby, and Gerry Cheevers with Elizabeth and Elsie Brazilian.

NOTABLE LOCALS

JAMES MICHAEL CURLEY (1874-1958)
~~GOV~~ERNOR OF MASSACHUSETTS, 1935-1937

~~James~~ Michael Curley is one of the enduring figures in ~~Massachusetts~~'s political history. After serving on various municipal ~~boards~~ and a single term in the Massachusetts House of ~~Repres~~entatives (1902-1903), he was elected to the U.S. ~~Congre~~ss (1911-1914).

~~After his~~ term in Washington, Curley returned to Boston, and ran for Mayor without the aid of the traditional political establishment. Though his opponents could not deny him election to the Mayor's office, they passed a law prohibiting election to consecutive terms. He would go on to win three terms - every other four years (1914-18, 1922-26, and 1930-34), and after reelection to Congress (1943-1945), he returned for a final term as Mayor 1945-1949. Mayor Curley was convicted of mail fraud in 1947. He served five months in prison during his final term as Mayor before receiving a Presidential commutation of his conviction and later a Presidential pardon.

After three terms as Mayor, he was elected Governor. While in office he accelerated the investment of millions of federal and state dollars in public works projects and induced regulated industries, such as banks and utilities to lower rates. He advocated for conservation projects, a 48-hour workweek and improved pension laws. Governor Curley declined to run for reelection in 1938 and ran an unsuccessful campaign for a seat in the U.S. Senate. After a subsequent failed Mayoral campaign, he returned to Congress (1943-1945), and then again to the Mayor's office (1945-1959).
(Adapted from mass.gov.)

Curley, who had a summer ~~ho~~me in Minot, frequently dined at the hotel.

MA~~URICE TOBIN~~ (1901-1953)
GOV~~ERNOR OF MASSACH~~USETTS, 1945-1947

Born i~~n a working-class ne~~ighborhood, Maurice Tobin attend~~ed Boston College befor~~e working for Conway Leather and New E~~ngland Tel~~ephone.

A protégé of James Michael Curley, Tobin was elected to the Massachusetts House of Representatives at age twenty-five. After serving on Boston's school committee from 1931-1937, he shocked the political establishment by challenging and beating his mentor, James Curley, in the 1936 Mayoral race.

Tobin served as Mayor of Boston from 1937 until he was elected Governor in 1944. He advocated the Fair Employment Practices Bill, which prohibited discrimination based on race, color, creed, and national origin in hiring or promotion practices. He described discrimination as a hideous evil which must be eliminated as a prerequisite to world peace.

Governor Tobin advanced bills to increase the benefits of Unemployment Insurance and Workers Compensation. He was defeated in his first reelection bid by Robert Bradford. Mr. Tobin remained active in Democratic politics, supporting Harry Truman for President and was appointed as his Secretary of Labor, serving from 1948-1953. *(Adapted from mass.gov.)*

Governor Tobin had a home in Scituate, and was a member of Hatherly Country Club. After his sudden death in 1953, the club founded the prestigious Annual Governor Maurice J. Tobin Memorial Member-Guest golf, which is held every August.

THOMAS P. "TIP" O'NEILL, JR. (1912-1994)
MASSACHUSETTS HOUSE OF REPRESENTATIVES
1936–1953
MASSACHUSETTS REPRESENTATIVE IN CONGRESS
1953–1987
MAJORITY WHIP 1971–73, MAJORITY LEADER 1973–77
SPEAKER OF THE HOUSE 1977–1987

"Tip" O'Neill was elected to the Massachusetts House of Representatives in 1936 just one year after graduating from Boston College. In 1949 he became its first Democratic Speaker. In 1952 he was elected to the congressional seat vacated by Senator-elect John F. Kennedy. He served with long-time Massachusetts Congressman John W. McCormack (Speaker from 1962-1971), and Edward M. Kennedy, who entered the Senate in 1962.

With powerful allies, O'Neill, an outspoken liberal Democrat, rose quickly through the ranks, gaining national attention with his early opposition to U. S. involvement in the Vietnam War and his support of the impeachment of President Richard Nixon.

He sponsored the bill that created the Cape Cod National Seashore Park (1961), and as Speaker was instrumental in bringing the "Big Dig" to Boston. He served until his retirement in 1987—fifty years after he entered public service. In 1991 he received the Presidential Medal of Freedom. *(Adapted from mass.gov.)*

> *Our House Speaker, Tip O'Neill, with a large party, was one of the frequent patronizers of our Sunday buffet.*
>
> *(Excerpt from Aram, Sr.'s autobiography)*

EDWARD ROWE SNOW (1902-1982)

A daily columnist at the *The Patriot Ledger* newspaper in Quincy from 1957-82, Edward Rowe Snow is widely known for his stories of pirates and other nautical subjects.

Descended from a long line of sea captains, Snow spent the decade following his 1919 graduation from high school working on oil tankers and sailing ships.

He went on to study at Harvard and Boston Universities. His BU master's thesis provided the foundation for his first book, "The Islands of Boston Harbor," in 1935.

Snow wrote more than 40 books and many shorter volumes. In all, he authored over 100 publications, mainly about New England coastal history. An avid student of New England maritime history, Snow established himself not only as a respected historian, but as a popular storyteller, lecturer, preservationist, and treasure hunter as well.

He also is fondly remembered for carrying on the tradition of the "Flying Santa," (begun by pilot Bill Wincapaw, who devoted ten years to the role) for over forty years, from 1936 until 1980. Every Christmas he would hire a small plane and fly along the coast from Maine to New York, dropping wrapped gifts to dozens of lighthouse keepers and their families.

In August 2000, in honor of Snow's tireless preservation efforts in the 1950s, a memorial was dedicated at Fort Warren, George's Island in Boston Harbor, which is now a public park. The Boston Harbor Cruise ferry Edward Rowe Snow was named in his honor as well.

I remember Mayor Curley, Governor Tobin and Edward Rowe Snow all visited the hotel.
Aram Brazilian, Jr., 2012

PERSONAL MEMORIES

**Our thanks to the folks whose summer adventures
included the Cliff Hotel for sharing those remembrances.**

CLIFF HOTEL — MINOT, MASS.

PERSONAL MEMORIES: FORMER EMPLOYEES

Barbara Griffin Kane ◆ Summers of 1960 & 1961

FASHIONS by MADELEINE'S of North Scituate were shown at the weekly fashion show by the pool at the Cliff Hotel Sunday, to quote owner Aram Brazilian; 'Aram and his Harem' Models are Barbara Griffin, Ann Misner, Paula McDonough, Mary B. and Liz Balir; (back row) Madeleine O'Neill and Mr. and Mrs. Brazilian.

The first year I worked at the Cliff Hotel, I was a waitress, and the next year I was the hostess. My future husband was the bartender in the Bamboo Lounge. You had to go through the snack bar to get into the lounge. I would be all dressed up and would go sit in the snack bar and wave at him because help was not allowed into the lounge. We used to go across the street to the beach. There was a grille on the patio that made hamburgers and hot dogs and you could sit out on the patio and eat.

◆

I was in charge of the girls *(waitresses)*. We had a term: "water and roll them," which meant to bring the customers water and a roll and butter, so if you were busy, they would have something to drink and eat until you could get back to them.

◆

Every Sunday there was a buffet, and they would serve lobster tails. We lived in "The Zoo," *(where a number of employees lived)*, and on Sunday after the buffet, we would bring the leftover lobster tails down to the Zoo. It was fabulous on Sundays.

◆

Tip O'Neill used to come in every Sunday. He got me my first job teaching. He asked me where I was going to teach; I lived in Belmont, so I told him I would teach in Belmont. He said, "No, you won't, you need some years of experience." And he wrote a letter recommending that I be hired as a teacher in the Watertown School District.

◆

I had to dress up every night, and I used to go to the Bargain Center in Quincy to buy my dresses. One time, when I went with my mother, I found a silver dress with spaghetti straps. The tag said 39 cents. The woman at the counter said it was a mistake and it should be $39.00, and my mother said, "It says 39 cents." So I got the dress for 39 cents.

PERSONAL MEMORIES

Barbara Griffin Kane ◆ Summers of 1960 & 1961

Julius La Rosa, who was starring at the Music Circus, came into the dining room and asked me if there was a church in the area. I told him there was a chapel around the corner. When he asked me if I was Catholic – and I said yes - he asked if I would go to church with him on Sunday. (The chapel was behind the hotel a few streets over. Today it's a home.) On Sunday, he came downstairs wearing a white shirt and screaming red pants! Nobody wore red pants back then. But I went off to church with him, and thought I was the cat's meow because I was going to church with Julius La Rosa!

Aram would say, "Now Barbara, I want all of you girls to get together - we are going to have a fashion show around the pool and you are all going to be the models. We would have parties, do skits, and have Hawaiian dances and parade all around the pool.
In this photo, my father is in the suit and I'm next to him.

When I had heard that the Cliff Hotel had burned to the ground it was a like a death in the family.

PERSONAL MEMORIES: FORMER EMPLOYEES

Dotty Tyler ◆ Summers of 1953 & 1954

Dotty (L) and Liz, a coworker.

During my first years in college, my friend Pat Merritt and I worked as Dieticians. During the summers of 1953 and 1954, between our sophomore and junior years, we decided we wanted to work at the beach. The first day we arrived *(at the hotel),* we were dropped off in the middle of a Nor'easter. It was cold and wet. Our room had bunk beds and there were three of us. We lived on the first floor of the house the first year and moved up to the second floor in our second summer.

We were paid $350 for the season with free room and board. The waitresses, waiters and other staff had to pay for their board.

Pat, Gail (Aram Brazilian's daughter) and I ran the coffee shop by ourselves. Pat and I were attending Framingham State College for the Food and Nutrition Program, which is perhaps why we were hired. The coffee shop was open from mid-morning until the bar closed. The Chef would give us the food to serve, including hamburgers, hot dogs and milkshakes, and at one point we started selling Westerns. We also had a grille and tried fry baskets, but that was not terribly successful.

When we were not working we would walk from Minot to the theater in the harbor - if you wanted to see a movie, you walked. Hatherly Road was long!

You had to walk through the coffee shop to get into the bar called the Bamboo Lounge. A band played in the bar every night. They would ask us what songs we liked, and they would play them for us every night.

During my first summer, a man came into the coffee shop heading to the bar for a beer. He thought he had seen me at a party the night before. We started talking and that was it: I'd met my future husband, Cliff. Cliff went into the service; this was during the Korean conflict. The war was over and he was in a reserve unit. I went back to school in the fall and we wrote to each other. I went to study at Beth Israel after my second summer working in the coffee shop. I graduated in 1954 and we were married that fall.

I enjoyed myself, I had a nice summer and I met my husband. I never would have met him if it weren't for the Coffee Shop at the Cliff Hotel.

Liz in Uniform

**Co-workers
Pat, Liz and Janet**

**Pat, Dotty and Liz
at Minot Beach**

Ken, one of the bellhops

**PHOTOS COURTESY OF
FORMER EMPLOYEE
DOTTY TYLER**

**Sailboat ashore in front
of the Cliff Hotel**

Glades Beach

Photos courtesy of
former employee Pat Merritt, 1953-1954

View of hotel from the parking lot.

Employees enjoying the beach.

Cliff Hotel employee residence, "The Zoo."

Freddie, chef's assistant; another kitchen employee; and head chef, Nick.

Waitresses and chambermaids
relax on Minot Beach.

Freddie catches his rays in
the parking lot.

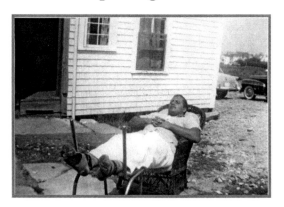

PERSONAL MEMORIES: FORMER EMPLOYEES

Richard Darling
Summer of 1964

I worked at the Cliff Hotel in the summer of 1964 as a dish/pot washer. All of us lived in a house behind the hotel that we called "The Zoo," and these are pictures of our gang. I can't remember many of them; I guess I was washing dishes while they were partying!

Rob Laney (left) and Richard Darling

My positive memories are with my very special girlfriend, Mary- Jo. There was a huge storm, and Mary-Jo and I walked down to the high wall that separated the road in front of the hotel from the beach. As we approached, we noticed that the ocean was not way down below at the entrance to the beach, it was crashing into the TOP of the wall and the impact waves were going as high as the hotel's rooms. We retreated to the comfort of our living quarters. (*Richard lived at the Zoo.*)

Billy *(a coworker)* played Bob Dylan's *Freewheelin'* album, which had just been released the year before in 1963, all night long. My bed was in the room next to Billy's (all of our rooms were very small and two of us lived in each). This innocent Vermont boy thought both Billy and Dylan were nuts, but, by the end of the summer, I was a Billy and Dylan fan, and after arriving at Syracuse University to start my freshman year I bought a guitar and started playing Dylan songs, which I play on stage to this day.

R: Beloved Chef Scotty, August 1964

L: Wally (on the left) was 2nd Chef to Scotty (on the right); Billy (center) was the salad man.

Christmas in August at The Zoo thanks to Chef Scotty Claus

MORE PHOTOS FROM RICHARD DARLING

Actors Joan MacIntosh and James Cromwell played at the Music Circus in 1964, and graciously posed for this photo.

Rare photo of Cliff Hotel Swizzle Sticks

THE SUMMER OF '64 "GANG"

Mary Beth Finan and Dave Polansky ↓

MUSICAL MEMORIES

The Cliffside Five 1963-1965

Thanks to Richard Darling, we do have one photo of The Cliffside Five, taken in at a party in The Zoo in 1964. The musicians, from left to right, are Bob Derbacher, Dave Polansky, Steve Richardson Roger Cahoon and Bob Lombard.

Dave Polansky, now an award-winning performer and composer, was kind enough to provide some background info on the group:

The Cliffside Five began when Bob Lombard (Guitar), Steve Richardson (Piano/Banjo), Bob Derbacher (Bass), and Herve LeBoeuf (Drums), all freshmen in the class of 1965 at Tufts University, got together sometime around the start of their freshman year and decided to form a band. Because Tufts is located on Medford Hillside, they called the band the Hillside Five.

They needed a horn player, but couldn't find a good match at Tufts. Bob Lombard and I were in high school together (though he is two years older) and we had been in a band together since I was in junior high school, so when no trumpet player could be found at Tufts, Lombard suggested that I join the band. (I was still a junior at Winthrop High School. We played fraternity parties, proms, etc. I was so excited to be in the company of those cool college dudes.) That's how it started.

The following spring we auditioned for the Brazilians, and were hired to play the summer at the Cliff.   They changed our name from Hillside Five to Cliffside Five. We worked seven nights a week and spent our days relaxing on Minot Beach which, back then, was wide enough to accommodate good size crowds. I think the ocean has swallowed most of it since then. It was a dream job for me and, I think, for the rest of the guys.

Herve, our drummer, was enrolled in Navy ROTC and was to become a fighter pilot and could not be at the Cliff for the entire summer. We needed someone to fill in, and (Scituate resident) Roger Cahoon took Herve's place. We absolutely loved his playing, his singing and his personality. We were lucky. It was a great fit.

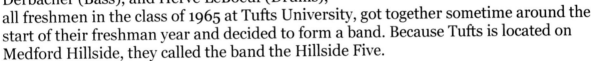

CLIFF *hotel* *"News Notes"*

July 11, 1963: I am pleased that the Cliff Side Five have won such general acclaim in so short a period. Their folk singing and versatile dance music is heard seven nights a week in the Bamboo Lounge.

MUSICAL MEMORIES

The Field of Zaad 1970

The musicians in the group are pictured here, clockwise from the top left: Bob Heiligmann, (drums/vocals) Jack Ross (guitar/vocals), Jeff York (vocals/flute) Elyse Thierry (vocals/bass) and Michael Workman (keyboards/vocals)

Michael generously shared some photographs from their summer at the Cliff; this excerpt is taken from his website, mikeworkman.com.

In the late spring of 1970, the five vocalists/ musicians that made up **The Field of Zaad** ... got the call to do a two-week gig in a resort hotel in Scituate, MA called the Cliff Hotel. It was very old, large, wooden Cape Cod architecture, right across from the beach.

The owners of the hotel liked the band from the start (and) offered The Field of Zaad a gig for the summer. This was truly a summer that is still very special in my mind. Besides a very steady paycheck, we were also given rooms at the hotel ... something we screwed up in the first couple of weeks we were there. One of the band members had a lack of indiscretion and the band had to find another place to stay.

We'd made friends with regular customers who came to see us. Some of the best friends our band had were Wendell and Diane. When they found we needed a place to stay, they rented the *Rose Cottage* to us.

As I said, it was a summer to remember. The days were as enchanting as the nights. Sure, I'd been to the beach before, but we were LIVING there now. We were feeling pretty good about everything Zaad. But nothing lasts forever. I was lucky enough to invite my mom and dad to see us on our last night. We had the crowd into the music, we thought we were keeping our volume down, but we were playing too loud. That was our last night of playing at the Cliff Hotel. We packed up our equipment that night, got a U-Haul the next day, and our endless summer ended.

Three wise humans: Bob Elyse and Jack behind behind the Cliff at 6 a.m.

"Mike on the rocks"

Bob in his favorite beach attire

PERSONAL MEMORIES: SCITUATE FOLKS

(Left to Right) Kate Mahony, Dorothy Sullivan, Ellen Mahony, Gina Sullivan, Kitsy Cavanaugh, Ann Sullivan, Gael Sullivan & Susan Connolly.

Here are my mother and friends back in the 1950s, enjoying
a celebration on the Cliff Hotel porch.
The thing I miss most about the Cliff Hotel is the clock.
We all used it to know when it was time to go home from the beach.
Gael Daly

PERSONAL MEMORIES: SCITUATE FOLKS

THE CLOCK

Although I have many great memories of The Cliff Hotel, there is one that clearly sticks in my mind.

As a young child in the 1950s, my sister, Barbara, my mother, Rita, and I would spend all day at North Scituate Beach with the Monahan Family.

The Monahans lived just two houses down from the entrance to the beach and we usually sat in front of the Sawyer's house.

When it got to be late afternoon, we would always have one eye on the huge clock that was on the front of The Cliff Hotel, hoping that it wasn't time to leave, just yet.

As the hands moved toward the time to go home, my mother would bribe us to leave peacefully by offering to stop for ice cream at The Snackery on Hatherly Road. I have a feeling that she wanted one as much as we did.

Christine DeStefano McKenna

Minot Beach, across Glades Road from the beach — you could see the clock from here! *nmy*

90

Personal Memories: Scituate Folks

One of my memories of the Cliff Hotel was a Scituate Rotary Club anniversary celebration in the late 1960s - early 1970s, when I was President. It was a big bash with a great band. The room was gorgeous, and there was a lot of fancy food, including lobster. It was a beautiful place that held all kinds of functions. A dear friend of mine who owned a deli on Front Street supplied the bread and rolls to the Cliff Hotel, as well.

I also had a connection to the entertainers who stayed at the Cliff Hotel and performed at the South Shore Music Circus ... I built the original two buildings for the Music Circus. The management took me down to the Melody Tent in Hyannis to show me the buildings and designs to follow for the Cohasset venue. I built two buildings ... one of them had no posts, so the room was open for rehearsals and dancing. I had to use special beams from Grossman's Lumber, as well as special wolmanzied lumber from Maine for the seating. I remember seeing many entertainers including Rich Little and Bob Hope.

I went through the building a few times. It was amazing how big it was. There was nothing like it back then. It was old, very old. I remember sitting on the front porch with the ocean in front of me, and a beautiful breeze. Just a beautiful place to sit, eat, and enjoy yourself.

Donn Sladen

I had my Quincy High School, Senior Prom (Class of 1950) at the Cliff Hotel.
Geraldine Mack Lind

PERSONAL MEMORIES: SCITUATE FOLKS

We live in Norwell now, but I am still a Minot "summer bum," with a family beach house located in the Glades Road section between the Adams estate/private property and the "low seawall." I remember the "Cliff" from my childhood (I also worked for three summers at another former Minot landmark, Susanne's Guest House).

What I remember is the huge main/side door (I recall it taking more than one of us to open it) that led to the lobby and staircase. In the late sixties/early seventies, one of the biggest TV stars in the country was Bob Hope; we spent a night or two going in and out of the lobby (and being asked to leave shortly thereafter) trying to get a glimpse of this big star, as we had heard that he was staying there while performing at the SS Music Circus..... never did see him.

Another memory is having a summer bum friend whose dad was a doctor with five kids and their family had a summer "membership," which allowed me to frequently accompany my friend to the pool and snack bar. The pool was across the street from the main building with a chain link fence around it, and it always seemed crowded, despite having such a big beautiful beach right across Glades Road. We could get a burger or ice cream from the snack bar and simply say, "put it on Dr. Reilly's tab." Leaving our neighborhood to go up to the Cliff for a few hours seemed like the coolest thing for a kid - which it was.

Also recall having the owner's sons pointed out to me, and being told they were the "Brazilians," which to a 10, 11 year old meant that they were from Brazil. Later on I found out that their surname was Brazilian (meaning they were Armenian).

Finally, I remember hearing about my older brother and his friends going to the Bamboo Lounge to drink beer (I think the legal age was 18 for a brief period back then) and dance/socialize with young women from Scituate, and guests from anywhere (heard of one night where they met young ladies from Kentucky). We couldn't wait to have our own Bamboo Lounge experiences, but, unfortunately, the grand Cliff Hotel burned to the ground well before we got to the legal age.

Bill Murphy

PERSONAL MEMORIES: SCITUATE FOLKS

I moved to Scituate in 1959, at the age of four...we lived on Old Farm Road, off Hatherly...in the early years, my mom was a stay-at-home mom with six kids... our main source of entertainment in the summer was the beach. On every sunny summer day we would walk down to N. Scituate beach, where we would spend blissful hours swimming, taking town-provided swimming lessons, building sandcastles and exploring the beach. When I was 8 or 9, my mother would allow us to go off on our own, as long as we kept an eye on the large clock outside the Cliff Hotel, to make sure we returned in time to go home for lunch. As a young girl, I assumed the clock on the hotel existed for just that reason, so kids would know what time to meet back with their Moms.

I remember my father chatting with a couple of the college aged girls who worked at the hotel one summer...working at the Cliff hotel was the first trip to Massachusetts for many of them, and in those pre-internet days, they knew very little about the hotel where they'd be spending the summer...as my father told us, they were given the impression that Scituate was "the gateway to Cape Cod," and were surprised to find that it was a wee bit further from Cape Cod than suggested.

When I got a little older, about 12 or 13, I babysat for people who were in town for the annual Tobin Tournament at Hatherly Country Club. I remember taking the children for a swim in the hotel pool, and then putting them to bed and waiting for the parents to return...it was my first time (and probably the last) babysitting in a hotel room! During one of the days that I babysat the children, I walked right past Jo Anne Worley of Laugh-In fame, sitting on the hotel's front porch, fanning herself. I was so star struck, and wanted to say hello, but she looked terribly cross, so I walked by without a word.

Another time my older brother Danny took me to the snack bar on the bottom floor of the hotel. I distinctly remember this visit, because I had been thrown while horseback riding earlier that day. He introduced me to my first fried clam that day, and as I found out later, they do not mix well with a chocolate shake. Apparently, I had suffered a slight concussion while riding, which caused me to throw up once we got home. I laugh when I think about it now, but I could not bring myself to eat a fried clam ever again.

My last memory of the hotel was the night it burned down. I was at Salvador's restaurant in Cohasset on Route 3A, when someone came in and said the Cliff Hotel was on fire. I remember seeing a huge orange glow in the sky as we drove towards Minot. When we got to the lights at Hatherly and Gannett, we walked the rest of the way and just stood on Glades Road, watching it burn. It was the first building fire I'd ever seen, other than on television, and a sight I'll never forget.

Joan Reid

PERSONAL MEMORIES: SCITUATE FOLKS

Greetings from St Augustine, Florida.
My name is Edward McCarthy, former resident of Scituate, with various ties to the Cliff Hotel ... lots of folks like myself have memories of enjoying cool beverages served from the bar!

But I alone have the following memory:

It was a cold March morning and I was heading north on 3A through North Scituate to do an errand in Cohasset.

As I passed Gannett Road, I observed two men on ladders taking down the remains of the old and faded Cliff Hotel sign. I say old and faded - the year was 1970. I stopped and shouted to them - would they like a hot cup of coffee? Yes, was the reply. When I returned, they were back on the ground loading scraps and pieces onto their truck.

They grabbed for the coffee and muffins with big smiles and thanks. When I asked what was to become of the two tin panels with the Cliff Hotel name on them, they said they were headed for the landfill. When I asked if I could take them home, they said sure, help yourself.

These two panels, for those who can't remember, were scaled down and set out in a third dimension as copies of what stood at the beginning of the walkway into the hotel. Both panels showed signs of being stoned and shot at but the gold leaf lettering was still in pretty good shape.

I shared one of the panels with a good friend; it is still in Scituate. The other panel is in Carver, at my son Christopher's house.

Edward McCarthy

Strike Box 414 - May 23, 1974

A general alarm fire whipped by cold wind blasts off North Scituate Beach destroyed the 75-year old Cliff Hotel and an adjacent home only one night before the hotel was to open for the summer.

The unoccupied, 125-room rambling wooden structure, was already engulfed in flames when the first Scituate firefighters arrived at the scene shortly before 10:00 p.m.

The following is a chronological and detailed account of that tragic night.

Courtesy of Captain Mark Donovan,
Scituate Fire Department

SCITUATE FIRE DEPARTMENT
FIRE REPORT

Still Alarm_____   NO. 412_____

Box Alarm No. 44_____   Date May 23,1974___

Alarm receive by: Telephone X___   Police Radio_____

                     Street Box X___   Verbal   _____

Location Glades Road - Cliff Hotel - Occupied home_____

Owned by James Claypoole - James Conant_____

Occupied by Hotel None - Home occupied by schoolteachers

Insurance on Building_____ Estimated damage Building_____

          Contents_____   Contents_____

> Every engine, rescue and car responded to the fire.

Time of Alarm_____a.m.9:41 p.m.   Time Out_____a.m.8:37 p.m.5/24/74

Time of: Working Fire 9:45pm Second Alarm 9:52pm Third Alarm 9:58pm___

Fire Alarm Operator D.Duffey - D.Quinn_____ Group No. 2 - 3____

Apparatus   X Engine 1 X Ladder 1   Apparatus X Engine 1 X Ladder 1
Responding   X Engine 2 X Ladder 2   Used   X Engine 2 X Ladder 2
              X Engine 3 X Forest 1   X Engine 3 _ Forest 1
              X Engine 4 X Forest 2   X Engine 4 X Forest 2
              _ Engine 5 X Car 30   _ Engine 5 _ Car 30
              X Rescue   X Car 32   X Rescue   _ Car 32

Hose Booster_____ft.   Ladders   Time Pumping_____hrs._____min.
Used 1 1/8"_____ft.   Used
     1 1/2" 2,600ft.   _____ft. Smoke ejector used_____
     2 1/2" 13,700ft.   Salvage covers spread_____

Type of Alarm:

                X Building   _ Auto   _ Accident
    _ False   _ Brush & Woods _ Oil Burner   _ Resuscitator
    _ Dump   _ Boat   _ Rubbish   _ Miscellaneous

Cause of Fire under investigation_____

Reported to Fire Marshal X Date May 24,1974_____

Investigated by Lt. Mowles_____ Date May 24,1974___

First Company at scene Engine #2_____ Time 9:45pm___

First Arriving Officer Capt. Sylvester_____

(over)

At 9:41pm, a call was received from an unidentified women, to inform this department that there was a fire in a building at the rear of the Cliff Hotel.
Box 44 was being received at about the same time.
While enroute to the fire, I informed the fire alarm operator to strike box 414 Cliff Hotel soon as the fire alarm console had cleared.
While enroute to the fire, the present of smoke was in the area of Mann Hill Rd. and Hatherly Rd. approximately 3/4 of a mile from the fire.
Engine #2 which is **station** approximately 1/8 of a mile from the hotel was the first truck at the scene and immediately layed one (1) 2½" hose line from the hydrant into the truck. One (1) 2½" and two (2) 1½" hose lines were layed to the North rear of the hotel. This room one the North rear basement was fully involved and had spread up into the kitchen area.
At this time the fire was spreading fast to the upper floors and had burned out through the outside walls.
Two (2) 2½" hose lines were ran into the sprinkler connection on the South side.
The second and third alarms were ordered sounded and Electric and Gas Co. were called to shut off utilities.
Two (2) deck guns and one ladder pipe were set up in the rear.
One (1) ladder pipe and several 2½" lines were set in the front and one (1) deck gun.
The hotel was fully involved within approximately ½ hour after arrival and collapsed 3/4 to 1 hours time. This was a fast spreading fire.

The occupied home on the South side of the hotel ignited from the intense heat and fire. Damage to the home was severe as the side wall, roof, upper floor, was destroyed and water, heat and smoke damage throughout.
Occupants names are as follows;

Nancy Barber	Dennis Beaulein
Marie Cushing	Roy Tobin
Claudette Nadeau	John Grenhan
Evelyn Cushing	Joseph Sears

A town back hoe was at the scene the next morning to dig out around where the OS&Y valve was to inspect to see if the sprinkler was shut off. It was turned off. Also the pipe leading from the outside fire department connection had a large rusted hole in it.
Lt. Mowles of the State Fire Marshals office was at the scene the following morning.
A detail was left at the scene until 8:37pm the following day. 5/24/74

Trucks at the fire ;		2½" hose	1½" hose
Cohasset Engines	1-2-3 Ladder- Forest	3000'	
Hingham "	2-6-8-Ladder #2	1000'	
Marshfield "	6-2-Rescue-Forest	150'	
Hanover "	4-Rescue-Tanker	450'	600'
Hull "	3		
Scituate "	1-2-3-4-2s-Ladders1-2		
	Rescue-Forest #2-Car31	8250'	2000'
Norwell "	1-2 Total-	900'	
		13750'	2600'

Hingham Engine #4 at Station #1
Marshfield "   #3 "   "   #2
Weymouth   "   #6 "   "   #3

Robert M Sylvester
Captain Scituate Fire Dept.

Courtesy of Chief Brian Stewart,
Scituate Police Department

Scituate Police Department

Daily Log

Sheet No. 4

Thursday May 23   1974

9.40 P.M. Three calls on the Cliff Hotel on fire. Detailed car 61 &62.   hc

9.44 P.M. Pro Shop alarm. Detailed car 64.   hc

9.53 P.M. Mrs Murphy Wheeler Park calls re. her son is away and would like
           his house checked with the fire so close to his house. Told her
           when a car was free we would check the house. Stan Murphys.   hc

9.55 P.M. Sgt. Finnie car 64 re. Pro Shop is secure. Window open a little
           from the top but no entry can be made. Notified Mr. Dywer.   hc

10.17 P.M. Sgt. Finnie car 64 re. notify Walter Allen on water. Notified
           Mr. Allen.

10.18 P.M. Sgt. Duffey calls about fire and if needed. Did not know at the
           time.

10.20 P.M. Sgt. Coyle car 63 re. need more men. Notified Sgt. Duffey and
           had any men with monitors on to call.   hc

10.22 P.M. Play house calls for a bank escort. Detailed Off. Hallagren. hc

10.25 P.M. Sgt. Finnie car 64 re. call all the men in.   hc

10.32 P.M. Sgt. Finnie re. send the two ambulances. Officers Westcott, Stone
           with the Cad. and Officers Fallon, Griffin with the Pontiac. hc

10.35 P.M. Fire dept monitor re. woman having a heart attack at 25 Collier
           Ave. Notified Sgt. Coyle car 63. Cad. ambulance on the way.   hc

10.43 P.M. Sgt. Coyle car 63 re. have Cohasset P.D. block off Border St.
           Notified Cohasset P.D.   hc

10.45 P.M. Marshfield P.D. calls re. have Auxilary men if needed. Notified
           Marshfield to send the men.   hc

11.01 P.M. Mrs McDonald 237 Hatherly Rd. calls re. woman at her house thinks
           she ran over some one. Detailed Officer McAvenia.   hc

11.05 P.M. Chris Scott at the station re. had an accident with a Hingam fire
           truck on Gannett Rd. Gave him accident forms and to get in touch
           with Hingham Fire Dept. in the A.M.   hc

11.15 P.M. Angelos alarm comes in. Detailed Officer Hallagren.   hc

11.16 P.M. Mrs Elmo 67 Edith Holmes Dr. calls re. some one trying to get in
           the house. Car 65 with Officer Damon took the call.   hc

𝔖𝔠𝔦𝔱𝔲𝔞𝔱𝔢 𝔓𝔬𝔩𝔦𝔠𝔢 𝔇𝔢𝔭𝔞𝔯𝔱𝔪𝔢𝔫𝔱
Daily Log

Sheet No. 5

11.05 P.M. Chris Scott at the station re. had an accident with a Hingam fire
truck on Gannett Rd. Gave him accident forms and to get in touch
with Hingham Fire Dept. in the A.M.   hc

11.15 P.M. Angelos alarm comes in. Detailed Officer Hallagren.   hc

11.16 P.M. Mrs Elmo 67 Edith Holmes Dr. calls re. some one trying to get in
the house. Car 65 with Officer Damon took the call.   hc

11.20 P.M. Party calls re. accident in front of 547 F. Parish Rd. Norwell
P.D. taking the call.   hc

11.30 P.M. Finnies wrecker called for F. Parish Rd.   hc

11.32 P.M. Officer McAvenia portable re. accident area off Mann Lot Rd. hc

11.35 P.M. Kevin Sullivan at the station re. had an accident with a Hingham
Fire Truck on Glades Rd. Gave him accident forms and to contact
Hingham Fire Dept. in the A.M.   hc

The following book was presented to my father on his retirement party by Carl Sternfelt.
Charlie Curran

Chief Charles W. Curran,
Scituate Fire Department,
Town of Scituate.

Dear Chief Curran:

May I take this opportunity to thank you for your
kindness and co-operation during the past few years.
It has been a great pleasure for me to work with you
and the members of the Department.

Knowing that you were interested in having copies of
the photographs taken on the night of the great fire
at Cliff Hotel, this volume has been prepared. Rather
than selecting a few of the better photographs, I have
included a copy of each and every photograph taken at
the fire. Not having sufficient fire-fighting technical knowledge to properly caption the photographs, I
am leaving that to you.

On your retirement, I wish you all of the very best.

Sincerely,

Carl Sternfelt

November 21, 1974

PHOTO HISTORY OF THE CLIFF HOTEL FIRE OF MAY 23 -24, 1974

This volume of photographs and news clippings has been made available through the co-operation of the personnel of the Scituate Fire Department, and is presented to Chief Charles W. Curran at his testimonial dinner being held at South Shore Country Club, Hingham, Mass., on November 21, 1974.

In 1974, the Chief of the Department, Charles W. Curran, retired because of ill-health. The Chief was not only a capable man, but a helpful friend to all his men and certainly a credit to the Town of Scituate for his loyal and devoted service.

My father was Fire Chief in Scituate retiring April 1, 1974. Walter Stewart became Acting Chief and the Cliff Hotel Fire occurred 2 months later.

Charlie Curran

Chief Stewart (left) Captain Bell (right)

Back south west corner of building.

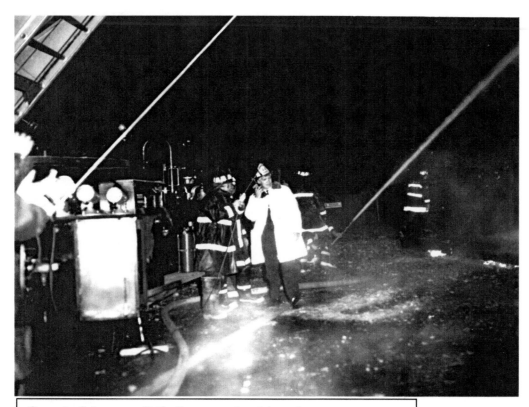

Captain Sylvester, Shift Commander (above)
Captain Sylvester and Firefighter George Cobbett (below)

Firefighters, John Dolan, Joe Fitzsimmons & Bart Curran (above)

"We first arrived at Scituate Headquarters providing Mutual Aid and then responded directly to the fire. Chief Walter Stewart was there - a great guy. We hooked up to the hydrant and felt we were spraying at something we were not going to save. I remember Chief Stewart coming up to me wondering where we could get more water. I actually considered pumping it from the swimming pool. There was also evidence that the fire was set in 4 different corners of the building. Statistics show that 96% of fires in buildings with sprinkler systems stay contained until the Fire Department arrives." At the time I was Captain of the Norwell Fire Department and later became Deputy Fire Chief.

Herb Fulton, Norwell, MA

We were working to protect the garage and house next door, when the stairs collapsed.   Charlie Curran

Alley where firefighters quickly escaped the collapse of the stairway.

Stairway that collapsed next to the garage.

Fire Department Chaplain (far left) with firefighters.

Captain Paul (Sonny) Kent

I was driver and pump operator on Engine 1. Engine 2 was the first engine in Minot. I went on the second alarm and the building was heavily involved.

Charlie Curran

This is a photo of my dad, Sgt. Robert W. Finnie, (1927-2010) of the Scituate Police, who was the first officer on the scene the night of the fire. He had been on patrol and was checking on the Hatherly Country Club when the call came in, so he was right in the neighborhood. I remember being on the phone with my boyfriend, who later became a firefighter, and I was debating whether to go to the fire or not. He wanted me to come and pick him up, as I had a car....and he was "on the way" from my house to "The Cliff."
I kept saying "it will be out by the time we get there...." He kept insisting I come and get him.....finally I did.....and needless to say, the fire was still blazing when we got there.
Thank God I didn't know that my father was there, or I would have been very worried for him. It was quite a night!

Ann Finnie, Scituate

Sergeant Robert Finnie, one of the first officers on scene.

Hingham and Hanover mutual aid engines.

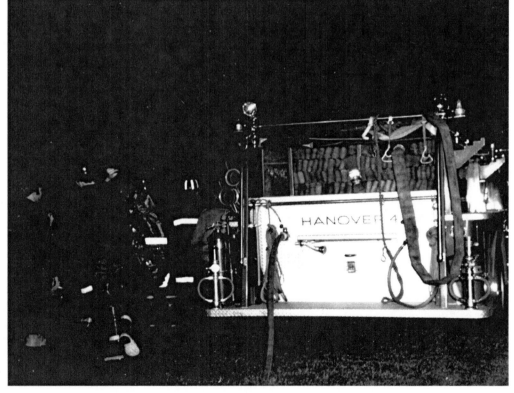

L. Stephen Sinnott, operating the deck gun on top of the engine, Stephen Kent, with his back to the camera - Marshfield Fire Department.

The Cliff Hotel the morning after.

When asked "How much fire did you have?
"We had plenty of fire for everybody" .
                              Charlie Curran

We were on scene overnight into the next day.
Charlie Curran

Back of building and pool area the next day.

Scituate's Rescue in the back of the building after the fire.

Thankfully, no lives were lost - civilian or firefighters.
Charlie Curran

Fire scene the morning after.

The Salvation Army provided coffee and donuts.

Hundreds of spectators gathered at the scene.

There was evidence that the OS&Y valve was shut off because the sprinklers weren't working.

Herb Fulton, Norwell Fire Department

Fire department connector to sprinkler system - evidence of rust and deterioration on pipe.

I lived about 3 blocks away on Hatherly Road and heard the fire horns sound the code for the Cliff Hotel. I could see the sparks in the air above my house, so I grabbed a camera and went down to see.

Larry Niland, Scituate

SCITUATE
FIRE FIGHTERS'
LOCAL 1464
BENEFIT

1974

Compliments Of

Allan R. Wheeler Inc.

106 STOCKBRIDGE ROAD

SCITUATE, MASSACHUSETTS

Telephone 545-0612 - 0288

The Cliff Hotel Fire

On the night of May 23rd, the Cliff Hotel burned. Only a maximum effort by eight fire departments, averted what could have become a major disaster. Under the capable direction of acting Chief Walter Stewart, fire forces surrounded and confined the holocaust. Because of its' close proximity to the main structure, fire extended to an adjacent building. An aggressive attack with heavy stream appliances stopped the fire there.

Flames leaped high into the air and burning embers, some as large as softballs, showered down on surrounding houses. Additional hose lines were stretched to combat this problem.

In all, there were three alarms sounded. Approximately one hour after arrival of the first apparatus, the old landmark succumbed to the ravages of the fire and collapsed. At dawn the next morning, all that remained of the hotel was a smoking pile of rubble.

A total of twenty-eight pieces of fire apparatus were in action at the fire. Three additional pieces were held at various stations throughout town. Equipment from Cohasset, Hingham, Marshfield, Norwell, Hanover, Hull, and Weymouth, in addition to that of Scituate, saw service. Well over three miles of hose was used. Lines were run on nearly every street in the area.

Much more effective than words, are the photographs contained in this book. They are the work of Mr. Carl Sternfelt and show quite graphically, events as they were.

Scituate firefighter raises ladder at rear of structure.

Alley on north side of building is still passable but rapidly getting dangerous.

The northwest corner of the building has collapsed and the fire begins to mushroom through the main section.

Northwest corner of building completely collapses.

Alley on north side of building now is completely blocked by collapsed ruins.

Entire building has now collapsed, sending a shower of sparks and flames over the neighborhood.

Large residence on south side bursts into flames.

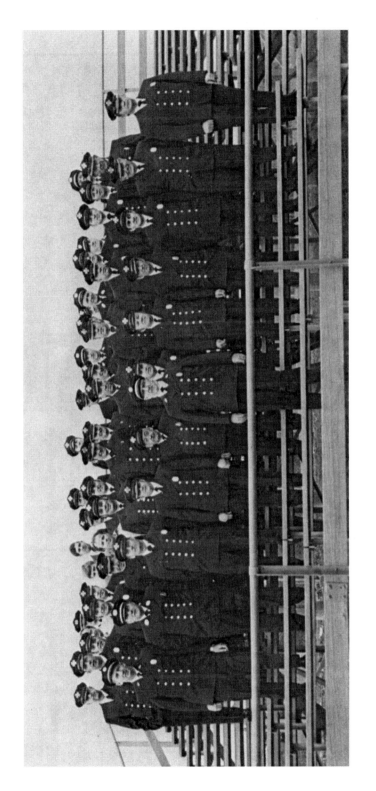

Scituate Fire Department - 1974

SPONSORS

J. J.'S
Rte. 3-A
Cohasset

BAKER'S 5¢ - $1.00
29 Main St.
Hingham

FINNIE'S SALES AND SERVICE
157 First Parish Rd.
Scituate

BURKHARDT BROTHERS
11 Mann Hill Road
Scituate

THE CARVING PLACE
Sea St.
Marshfield

BERGSON'S
Rte. 3-A
Cohasset

RAY'S REPAIR SHOP
364 Clapp Rd.
Scituate

SOUTH SHORE AMBULANCE
695 Jerusalem Rd.,Cohasset
383-0020

ABBADESSA SERVICE STATION
345 Rockland St.
Hingham

STAN MURPHY INSURANCE
14 Cherry Lane
Scituate

DONORS

PAYNE'S COLOR MART

HINGHAM OPTICAL
SHOPPE

KING JEWELERS

KEN BAILEY'S
PACKAGE STORE

SCITUATE MEDICAL LAB

THAYER PHARMACY

SCITUATE MUSIC

YOUNG'S BOAT STORAGE

C.W.K. - S.P. 1 & 2

VILLAGE BARBER

SHEEPSKIN BAY

CAPE COD PACKAGE
STORE

SIEMINSKI'S MOBIL
STATION

WOOLWORTH'S

TURNER'S PACKAGE
STORE

GEORGE CARCHIA &
SON

JAMES GODDARD

HINGHAM ANIMAL
HOSPITAL

R.M. BONGARZONE INC.

M.A. STREET INS.
AGCY., INC.

PETERSEN REAL
ESTATE

CUSHING HALL INC.

VILLAGE FABRICS

PAT'S HAIR STYLING
& BARBER

CAMP DANIEL WEBSTER
INC.

CLAY REAL ESTATE

HANCKEL ASSOCIATION

OKONITE CO.

FIVE SEASONS SPORT
SHOP

EUGENE BLANCHARD,
BUILDERS

SOUTH SHORE COUNTRY
CLUB

DWYER'S ONE STOP
CLEANERS

SIGNORELLIS RESTAURANT

GERTRUDE'S BEAUTY
STUDIO

T. R. STEARNS & SON

22

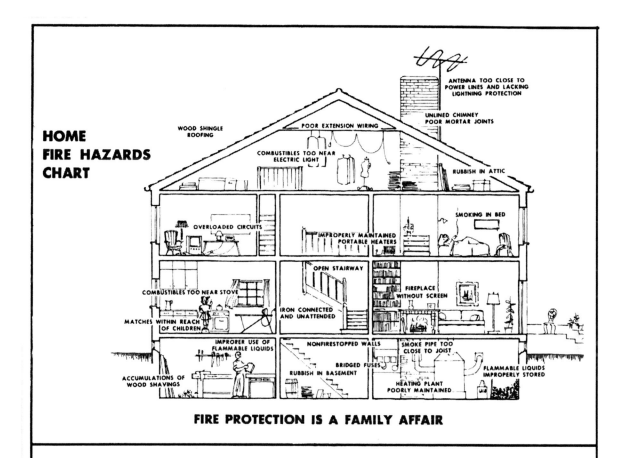

HOME FIRE HAZARDS CHART

ANTENNA TOO CLOSE TO POWER LINES AND LACKING LIGHTNING PROTECTION

UNLINED CHIMNEY POOR MORTAR JOINTS

WOOD SHINGLE ROOFING

POOR EXTENSION WIRING

COMBUSTIBLES TOO NEAR ELECTRIC LIGHT

RUBBISH IN ATTIC

SMOKING IN BED

OVERLOADED CIRCUITS

IMPROPERLY MAINTAINED PORTABLE HEATERS

OPEN STAIRWAY

COMBUSTIBLES TOO NEAR STOVE

FIREPLACE WITHOUT SCREEN

IRON CONNECTED AND UNATTENDED

MATCHES WITHIN REACH OF CHILDREN

IMPROPER USE OF FLAMMABLE LIQUIDS

NONFIRESTOPPED WALLS

SMOKE PIPE TOO CLOSE TO JOIST

BRIDGED FUSES

FLAMMABLE LIQUIDS IMPROPERLY STORED

ACCUMULATIONS OF WOOD SHAVINGS

RUBBISH IN BASEMENT

HEATING PLANT POORLY MAINTAINED

FIRE PROTECTION IS A FAMILY AFFAIR

FIRE CAN HAPPEN TO YOU

This very year, on the basis of national averages, a home in your general neighborhood will be involved in fire. It could be yours. Every minute of the day an American home is destroyed or damaged by fire. Every day, 17 people---mostly the young and the aged---die in these fires. Fire deaths occur when the simple rules of fire safety are violated---smoking in bed, leaving children alone in the house, allowing youngsters to play with matches.

More than half of each year's fire victims are killed by fires in their homes---more than those killed by all other fires combined. The yearly dollar cost to American home owners is over $300,000,000. But facts and figures can't describe the headache of fire damage to your home, the heartache of injury---sometimes death---which fire may bring. Every home represents a failure---failure to correct hazzards to take precautions.

SPONSORS

NICK'S GULF STATION
135 Front St.
Scituate

HARBOR TIRE MART & BIKE SHOP
5 Brook St.
Scituate

COUNTRY WAY RADIO & T.V.
786 Country Way
No. Scituate

CLAM HAVEN
Marshfield Ave.
Humarock Beach

HINGHAM LUMBER
190 Summer St.
Hingham

PITTS TRAVEL AGENCY
88 Front St.
Scituate

FREDRICKSON BROS.
Washington St.
Norwell

HARBOR BOOK STORE
Front St.
Scituate

COHASSET MOTORS
Rte. 3-A
Cohasset

WILDER BROS. TIRE MART
Country Way
No. Scituate

BUILDING 19
Lincoln St.
Hingham

J'S BEAUTY SHOPPE
Gannett Rd.
No. Scituate

HINGHAM OPTICAL SHOPPE
55 South St.
Hingham

THE COUNTRY FARE RESTAURANT
1217 Main St.
Hingham

EGYPT COUNTRY STORE
1 Curtis St.
Scituate

BROOKS PHARMACY
384 Gannett Rd.
No. Scituate

FIRST COUNTY NATIONAL BANK
Country Way
No. Scituate

VILLAGE SUB SHOP
778 Country Way
No. Scituate

MILL RIVER MARINE
Rte. 3-A
Cohasset

PIONEER WELDING, INC.
Building 39 - Lincoln St.
Hingham

SOUTH SHORE BUS, INC.
Building 54 - 349 Lincoln St.
Hingham

STOW-A-WAY SPORTS INDUSTRIES
166 Rte. 3-A
Cohasset

149

A grateful THANK YOU . . .

to these Sponsors for their assistance in the success of our Fund

DR. Thomas V. Serino
DR. Arch. T. Hodge
DR. J. E. Joyce
DR. Martin Geher
DR. Paul W. Rathbun
DR. Robert A. Seidel
DR. H. N. Blanchard
DR. James V. Shannon

DR. Clifford Ward
DR. Carl Pipes
DRS. Monsees & Smith
DR. Ralph Rogol
DR. John Dalco
DR. Ruth Bailey
DR. John F. O'Hara
DR. Max D. Miles

Abrahamson & Garside (ARCHITECT)
T. B. Hanna (ARCHITECT)

E. C. Labruque (C.P.A.)

ATTY. W. H. Obrenberger, Jr.
ATTY. Edward P. Ryan
ATTY. Wojcik
ATTYS. Price & Elliot

ATTY. Charles G. Simon
ATTY. John Webb
ATTY. Walter L. Sullivan
ATTY. Ralph Warren Sullivan

Thanks, to the members of . . . .

THE HUNDRED CLUB OF MASSACHUSETTS

ACKNOWLEDGMENT

I would like to thank, along with the members of the Scituate Firefighters Local #1464, the many advertisers, sponsors, and donors in this year's book for their most loyal support.

Without their support many of our projects would never be accomplished such as our annual School Scholarship. Personal thanks to Carl Sternfelt for his pictures which appear in this book; Capt. Fred Timpany for his write-up of the Cliff Hotel Fire; President Frank Hall, Ralph Butler for their aid and help; and last but not least, Dick Turner for his most needed assistance.

I thank you.

Stanton Merritt
Scituate Firefighter

NEWS!

- SOUTH SHORE MIRROR
- HINGHAM MIRROR
- HULL MIRROR

Serving:

- Cohasset
- Hanover
- Marshfield
- Norwell
- Pembroke
- Scituate

Published by:
**South Shore
Publishing Co., Inc.**
777 Country Way
North Scituate, Mass. 02060

THE

WELCH COMPANY

Gift Shop

SCITUATE HARBOR,
MASS.
TEL.
545-1400

Fire Destroys Cliff Hotel In Scituate

16—The Cliff House, Minot Beach, No. Scituate, Mass.

FIRE DESTROYS CLIFF HOTEL IN SCITUATE

Patriot Ledger South Edition May 24, 1974

SCITUATE - A general alarm fire whipped by cold wind blasts off North Scituate Beach last night destroyed the 75-year old Cliff Hotel and an adjacent home only one night before the hotel was to open for the summer.

The unoccupied, 125-room rambling wooden structure, was already engulfed in flames when the first Scituate firefighters arrived at the scene shortly before 10:00 p.m.

Our class - 1968 - had our senior banquet there. The night it burned my father got the call to go over and turn off the gas. He (Tommy Brown) worked for the Brockton Taunton Gas Company. We - Mom, Dad and the 5 of us jumped in the car and couldn't get any closer than the pond. We walked to the hotel and he went in amidst the flames to turn off the gas.

Heather Brown Colbert

Summer Resort

The summer resort for theater and movie stars, political figures and others over the years was valued at about $500,000.

Acting Fire Chief Walter M. Stewart was at an advisory committee meeting seeking a transfer of $3000.00 for repairs and gasoline for the fire department when he was notified of the fire.

He immediately called the station and ordered two more alarms rung and rushed out to the blaze.

Apparatus from Cohasset, Hingham, Hull, Weymouth, Hanover and Norwell were sent to the fire and scores of firefighters fought the blaze.

Flames and clouds of sparks at times reached near 100 feet into the air, spreading the fire to an adjacent home owned by the hotel owners, James Claypoole and James Conant of Clayton Development Corp.

Towers of flying sparks, visible as far as Weymouth, continued to threaten the entire Glades Road - Cherry Lane neighborhood even after the roof of the hotel building collapsed shortly after the third alarm.

Hundreds of spectators - some in pajamas - lined the banks overhanging North Scituate beach as firefighters doused homes as a preventative measure on either side of the hotel and the Claypoole-Conant house.

Early spectators said the fire apparently broke out in a rear kitchen section of the building and quickly spread through the main building and one of six cottages in the hotel complex.

The cottage closest to the main building was destroyed.

All that was left standing was a wall of melted aluminum siding arching toward the ocean. Owners of the hotel said that approximately 15 people were living in the six cottages and that all were evacuated before firefighters poured water over the buildings.

Cause Unknown

The building was equipped with a sprinkler system but chief Stewart said it was no match for the rapidly spreading blaze.

The cause of the fire is listed as undetermined and the state fire marshal's office has been asked to investigate.

No injuries were reported, said Chief Stewart, despite the intense heat and flying sparks.

This morning a handful of subdued bystanders watched firefighters spray isolated streams of water on the blackened rubble, as steam and light gray smoke rose gently from the smoldering ruins.

All that remained was a lonely centered chimney and a partially collapsed second one.

Heaps of charred timbers were enmeshed with twisted heating pipes and lying next to what was once the expansive front porch was a sign that simply read "Opening Memorial Day Weekend."

Scituate High School senior, Noel Soccorso of 44 Whittier Drive, visiting a friend three or four doors down the street from the hotel, said he and his companion smelled smoke about 9:30 or 9:45 p.m. They walked down a driveway near the hotel, he said, and seeing flames in the rear kitchen area ran back to a nearby house to call in the alarm. On returning to the hotel, he said they discovered the fire had already spread up the side of the wood-frame building, apparently fed by the cold sea-gusts.

The aluminum-sided house next to the hotel also owned by the two hotel owners was ignited shortly after the front porch and roof of the main building of the hotel collapsed sending spectators scurrying to safety.

> I will never forget the night it burned down! My Mum woke me, and my bedroom had a glow and the smell of fire. We took our family dog, Jenny, and walked the seawall as close as we could get. The hotel was fully engulfed. I could feel the heat of the fire on my face and watched as the front crumbled to the street.
>
> Judith Gordon, former Minot resident

Confined

The fire was finally confined to the hotel and Claypoole-Conant house area shortly before midnight, but officials expected firefighters to be at the scene for most of the day.

Spectator, Richard Bowen of Gannett Road, who was to start summer work as a maintenance man at the hotel today, said he arrived on the scene as the fire spread from the rear of the building. He and other spectators indicated they saw no one leave the building or the adjacent home, which they believed were unoccupied pending the opening of the hotel season today.

> Worked there with lots of friends through both ownerships.
> Pool house could tell lots of interesting stories if it could speak.
> Rusty Rosenberger

Noel Soccorso indicated however, that the hotel - often used for proms and banquets - had been the scene of a banquet earlier this week. Rep. George Young (R-Scituate), who was on hand to view the aftermath today, recalled the hotel hosted a Scituate Chamber of Commerce candidate's night last week, too.

Built in 1899, the hotel was sold to the Claycon Corporation in 1971 for $500,000. Prior to its sale to Hingham School Committee member, Claypoole and Mr. Conant of 48 Main Street, Hingham, the hotel was owned by Atty. Aram Brazilian for 29 years. Before that it was owned and operated by the Cushing family and then by the Summers family.

Renovated

Under the Brazilian's ownership the hotel was renovated in 1961 and a swimming pool installed. The Hingham Claycon Corporation continued renovations of the building.

Under the Brazilian's ownership the hotel had been host to many famous persons, including theater personalities Maurice Chevalier, Betsy Palmer, Zsa Zsa Gabor, Sid Caesar, Dan Daley, Imogene Coca, Julius La Rosa, Tom Poston and the late Hal March.

Former governor and Boston Mayor, the late James Michael Curley, also had lived at "The Cliff" until he purchased a summer home in North Scituate.

> As a kid, I recall hearing the fire horns blaring, nonstop. My father knew something really bad was happening. He put us in his truck and down to Hatherly Road we went. As fire trucks raced by, he knew which way to go ... and what had to be on fire to warrant so many calls for help. When we arrived, we smelled smoke, yet could not see any flames. Not too long after though, we did. We stayed until the whole thing was gone. It was beyond sad watching big sections of the building ... just collapse. A beautiful old period piece from grander days gone by ... gone in the virtual blink of an eye.
>
> Robert Jason

DEATH OF A LANDMARK, LIVELIHOOD

Patriot Ledger South Edition May 24, 1974

SCITUATE - For James Claypoole and James Conant, owners of the Cliff Hotel, the fire that destroyed the famed landmark was the death of a livelihood, but for the others it was more like the death of an old friend.

"Golden Egg"

James Claypoole of Scituate bought the hotel complex along with James Conant in 1971 for $500,000. "It was the goose that laid the golden egg and now it's gone," he said sadly. "We had functions booked every week, we were completely booked. I have no idea what we are going to do."

Mr. Claypoole, a Hingham school committee member, said that he could not possibly estimate how much money they've invested to build the place up for the grand opening this weekend.

James Conant said the hotel main building was insured for "about $500,000," but that the place was for him really "the whole hell in a handbag. Our bookings were up 40 percent from last year and we had already 70 or 80 bookings for the season. The energy crisis helped us in a way," he said.

Mr. Conant also said that he was glad no lives were lost because, "over a lifetime you can rebuild a building, but you can't rebuild a life." But, he said, they are going to honor their business obligations and try to find other places to rent to hold the functions they have booked. "We will use our own people to staff these functions and everything will be the same except for the location," he stated. Right now both owners are looking for a place to hold the two wedding receptions booked for the weekend.

Neil Murphy, Selectman chairman, has lived near the Cliff House all of his life and said that "the skyline is gone – a place you used to look at in the first part of the morning won't be there anymore."

Mr. Murphy remembered when he and Aram Brazilian, Jr. whose family owned the business for 29 years, used to study three nights a week in high school in the rooms of the hotel. "We would always be around the hotel working on one thing or another …. a new wall, a new bar ….anything and everything," he said.

> I was there the night of the fire. Lots of other memories - Jo Anne Worley and Tom Poston on the verandah. The Bamboo Lounge … sneaking into the pool with my dad, and, of course the great grilled cheese sandwiches in the snack bar … good times.
>
> Siobhan Foley

Cliff Hotel Fire Photos ... Pages 4 & 5

Scituate

mirror

thursday, may 30, 1974

volume 27
number 24
copy 15¢

THE CLIFF HOTEL DESTROYED BY FIRE!

Scituate Mariner, Thursday, May 30, 1974 by Gale Westcott

On the morning after, it looked like the circus had been in town. Salvation Army cups and food wrappers littered the street; the long throbbing snakes that had pumped thousands of gallons of water the night before were gone and hundreds of spectators paraded by to pay their last respects to the 76 year old Scituate landmark. The 125 room, rambling Cliff hotel was destroyed by a general alarm fire which began at approximately 9:30 pm. on Thursday, May 22.

Mr. and Mrs. Aram Brazilian Jr. were among the crowds that night as thousands watched the Cliff Hotel burn to the ground. "It was very sad as I watched my husband's face drain of color. We are shocked and devastated, the Brazilian family has spent 30 years in the big old hotel. Mr. Brazilian, Sr. purchased the hotel when Aram and his sister Gail were small children. John was born there, and Gail and I were both married there. Our son Aram III was born there also. It was always a happy place and we are extremely grateful that these memories are not marred by any deaths due to the fire," said Mrs. Elizabeth Brazilian.

According to Water M. Stewart, acting fire chief, apparatus from Scituate, Cohasset, Hingham, Marshfield, Norwell and Hull were at the scene. Two hundred and fifty firemen worked to get the blaze, which spread to an adjacent home, under control. The cause of the fire is listed as undetermined, however it was discovered during the investigation that the sprinkler system had been shut off. The building had recently been inspected by William Stone, town building inspector, and Chief Stewart, and a complete inspection had been scheduled for May 28.

Immediate reaction to the loss of the Cliff was unanimous. "Old things are very precious and the Cliff was one of the few grand hotels still operating," said one old-timer.
"I expected that place to go ten years ago," said one resident. "Where are the young kids going to go now for entertainment and getting together?" questioned Claire Cook. "The beach front will always look strange. It is just not the same," sighed an 80 year old woman who enjoys a morning walk on the beach.

After sentiments are put aside, the repeatedly voiced question is "What will come next?" A building that has been destroyed by fire or flood can be rebuilt under the zoning laws. In what form will the Cliff be rebuilt? Residents wonder if the North Scituate Beach front will become the site of a large motel or will it be condominiums? "I hope they don't stick some high rise condominium along our lovely coast," exclaimed a concerned citizen..

James Claypoole and James Conant who purchased the Cliff in 1971 for $500,000 stated that they have no present plans for reconstruction.

The Patriot Ledger

CLIFF HOTEL SPRINKLERS WEREN'T ON

Quincy Patriot Ledger, by Marilyn Jackson

The sprinkler system in the Cliff Hotel had been shut off when a general alarm blaze broke out in the 75 year old resort Thursday night, Acting Fire Chief Walter M. Stewart disclosed today.

Didn't Trip Alarm

Chief Stewart said the sprinkler system had not tripped the alarm to the fire station. When the department had arrived at the fire, the fire was in a very advanced stage, he said. "We hooked up into the sprinkler system and were unable to provide any pressure through the system. At the time we thought that an excess number of sprinkler heads had operated. After digging through the rubble, however, we retrieved the sprinkler valve, and it had been turned off."

"By law, the owner is required to notify the fire department when the valve is shut off. Perhaps the workmen had shut it off by mistake. In the past, the sprinkler service man has been very cooperative, more than cooperative, in letting us know when it was being turned off," Chief Stewart said. The water pipe inside the foundation wall which supplied the sprinkler system was badly corroded and "we were unable to feed it."

"The sprinkler system was an old system, no question about it," he said. "Whenever you have a sprinkler system in an old wood-framed building, there is a question of adequacy. The fire could go through the partitions or originate from the outside, and then the fire could extend to such proportions that it would overpower the sprinkler system," he continued.

Inspected Recently

William Stone, town building inspector, and Chief Stewart had gone through the hotel about three weeks ago on a state inspection and a full inspection had been scheduled for Tuesday. Bulldozing operations began yesterday, turning over the badly charred smoldering timbers as firefighters poured water onto the site of the North Scituate landmark.

The last fire truck returned to headquarters at 8:37 p.m. last night. Hundreds of spectators continued to be drawn to the scene of the spectacular blaze and children took souvenirs from the debris.

James Claypoole of Hingham, an owner of the hotel, met with Scituate town officials to determine how to dispose of the tons of debris in a town already overburdened with disposal problems.

The disposal will be done at no cost to the town. The owner's wrecking company will salvage as much as possible, including all metals and brick, which will considerably cut down the volume of debris, Edward G. McCann, Town Administer, said.

At Torrey Lane Pit

All ash, plaster and mortar will be buried at the site. What remains is wood, beams and charred material, and the town will permit it to be dumped at the town pit off Torrey Lane. It will be dumped in an excavated hole and covered, he added.

James Conant, the other owner of the hotel, said last night that two quotes attributed to him in yesterday's Patriot Ledger were reported incorrectly. Mr. Conant had been quoted in the paper as saying the hotel main building was insured for "about $500,00" but the place was for him really "the whole hell in a handbag."

"The $500,000 figure was taken out of context. There is the main building and several complexes - cottages." Mr. Conant would not comment on what the property was insured for at the time of the blaze.

He also clarified another point concerning staffing of future functions. He had been quoted in the paper as saying "we will use our own people to staff these functions and everything will be the same except for the location."

Mr. Conant said that statement should have read "we will be doing everything possible to find new locations for the weddings, banquets and class reunions."

Aram Brazilian Jr. of Cohasset, whose father was the previous hotel owner, said his parents in Florida "were all broken up" when he telephoned them about the resort's destruction. "You can't be involved with something for 29 years and not feel saddened when you lose it this way. My father bought the place in 1942 and I grew up with the place," he said.

The hotel was built in 1898 and was one of the last turn of the century Victorian buildings in this area, Mr. Brazilian said.

I remember the night it burned down. I was hired as a chamber maid for the cottages that remained out back after it burned down ... I made $2.00 an hour and rode my bike there. I was 13 or 14. We had a trailer out back for the office and supplies. The cottages ranged from a studio to a unit that slept 8 or more for families. It was me and one other girl whose name I can't remember. When we did a changeover for units, I had to clean the oven, which always took hours, and I hated it. I know my older sister used to sit on the patio bar for drinks.

Elizabeth MacKay

The Demise of the Cliff Hotel...

WHERE WILL SCITUATE YOUTHS GO?

By Claire Cook, Scituate Mirror, May 30, 1974

Since last Thursday Night, the fiery destruction of the Cliff Hotel has been a major topic of conversation for most Scituate residents.

Sympathetic murmurings for the Cliff's owners, predictions as to whose hands its business will fall into, and noddings of "I knew it would happen" abound in every corner of the town.

Where will the Bruins stay? And what about the Music Circus stars? Who will take over the wedding receptions and wealthy vacationing clientele?

There's another side to all of this, a side that is being characteristically ignored. What about the kids? Yeah - the older bracket of Scituate's youth - aged eighteen to somewhere in the twenties. The Cliff was their weekend haven last summer, a place where they could be with friends, have a few drinks and dance to a band like *The Shittons*.

Sure, drinks were overpriced, the dress code was strict, a few fights broke out over the course of the summer, but still the lounge at the Cliff Hotel was the one place that catered to Scituate's youth. Equivalent facilities seem reluctant to open their doors to masses of youth. Kids don't tip as well as adults, fights may occur, more bouncers are needed to weed out under-agers, older patrons will go elsewhere. All legitimate reasons but where does that leave Scituate's youth?

The townspeople of Scituate have already seen what can happen to kids given a summer of nowhere to go. The Egypt Beach incident of '72 should suffice as an example. Unsupervised beach parties en masse went out with the 50s. Be it the fault of police, residents, kids, or more likely a combination of the three, a summer of outdoor free-for-alls can only lead to trouble.

It seems that a new summer weekend entertainment spot for the young adults of Scituate is sorely needed. Not only would such a place benefit the youth of Scituate, but the older crowd could continue to appreciate their own style of weekend entertainment without the unwelcome invasion of younger people.

The lounge at the Cliff Hotel did much to keep both age groups happy. Memories of one short enjoyable summer are strong in the minds of Scituate youth. But now where?

FROM DONALD A. MAUCH, JULY 18, 2012

I grew up and resided at 16 Mann Lot Road from 1955 until 1975. My family would frequently spend time at Minot's Beach and became very familiar with the Cliff Hotel and the Brazilian family. Two or three years before the hotel's demise, my landscaping company, South Shore Lawn Care and Landscaping, was hired by the new owners, Jay Conant and Jim Claypool (ClayCon Development Corp.) to spruce up the property a week or so prior to the opening of each season.

The first year we were engaged, we replaced shrubs, raked the property and removed assorted debris that had accumulated throughout the winter. We spread mulch, and swept the common outside areas including the patio and walkways around the guest cottages. We took a lot of pride in freshening up the property each season, as it was one of our larger accounts. A week or so prior to the Memorial Day opening in 1974, I called Jay Conant to schedule our routine meeting to discuss the scope of work and to go over the various tasks that needed to be addressed. I distinctly recall that Jay was uncharacteristically evasive over the phone but was able to agree upon a date and time to meet with him.

Upon my arrival a few days later, and the day before opening, Jay appeared to be in a rush and was for the most part dismissive of my suggestions. In fact it was the first time that he rejected the idea of bringing in any new shrubs or mulch, which I recall as being most unusual. Our work was confined to raking up the surroundings, and sweeping the patio. Conspicuously, I along with two of my employees noticed upon entering the kitchen, that piles of dirty dishes, linens, and solidified grease in the fry-o-laters remained from the prior season. We were shocked at the filth and wondered why and how management expected to get the place in operating condition within a matter of hours before opening. We also noticed that the owners had just recently completed a new exterior paint job. Indeed, the impressions we received were very mixed messages as to what was going on.

That same evening as my Dad and I were watching TV, the fire horn began to blare. We had become quite accustomed to recognizing certain combinations of the horn and my Dad suddenly blurted out, "That's down Minot, the Cliff Hotel." It was a stormy and particularly windy evening with the wind blowing directly from the northeast. I immediately grabbed my coat, got into my car and headed for Minot down Country Way through North Scituate, and followed Gannett to Hatherly, meeting up with two of the Scituate Fire engines en route. I took a left onto Hatherly, staying clear of the fire engines and at the end turned right down Bailey's Causeway towards the Glades.

I pulled over just opposite Susanne's Guesthouse and could not believe what I was witnessing. It occurred to me that I was among the first of Scituate's residents to be witnessing this event.

The fire engines were just converging upon the site and I could see from my vantage point from across the salt marsh three (3) distinct and separate small fires roughly equidistant from each other on the first floor from the front portion, to the center, and to the rear.

The stiff winds off the ocean fanned the flames such that it became rather obvious that the Cliff Hotel was in dire trouble. Sadly, the aftermath became history although the intrigue as to the cause of the fire would continue.

Ironically, at the time, my Dad and I were in the process of replacing a rotted foundation sill on our old barn. Before the days of the Home Depots and Lowes and pressure-treated wood, I recall my Dad wondering where we could get a seasoned piece of sill that measured 8"x8"x12'.

Without hesitation, I suggested that perhaps there was one left in the debris of the burned out Cliff Hotel. I placed a call to Jay Conant and asked if I could take a look to determine if there was a salvageable portion. Much to my surprise, Jay asked me to bring a couple of hundred bucks and meet him at the site at around 11 P.M. at night, telling me that that was the only time he had available. So, at quarter to 11 P.M. I gathered up my Dad's chain saw, hooked the trailer to my car and set off for what remained of the Cliff.

The experience was surreal, with Jay pulling up in complete darkness in his red Cadillac (El Dorado as I recall) and with his headlights aimed across what was left of the foundation, told me to "hurry up." I recall finding a portion of sill and frantically cutting through metal spikes with my Dad's chainsaw, thinking what trouble I was going to get into by ruining the chain. All the while, Jay kept telling me to "hurry up," otherwise he was going to have to get going. Unfortunately, time was not on my side and I was forced to abandon the pursuit. Later I would discover an explanation for Jay's impatience and our cloak of darkness.: ClayCon's insurance company had already secured the remains of the site and whatever little salvage was left, legally belonged to them.

Shortly afterwards, word started to spread around town that the Scituate Fire Department, only days before, had paid the "Cliff," a visit for its annual inspection, but that inexplicably on the night of the blaze, it was discovered that the hotel's sprinkler system had been shut off. I believe this is what might have prompted the State Fire Marshall's office to suspect arson.

Eventually as I recall, an investigation was started ... I believe that both partners were eventually cleared by the authorities, though I have always believed that because of the circumstantial evidence from Jay Conant's evasive and dismissive behavior the day before opening, to the leftover grease in the fry-o-laters and dirty dishes and linens, to the sprinkler system that had been shut off, to the windswept conditions of that evening, arson was involved.

(Editor's note: This is a personal statement submitted by Donald Mauch, who currently resides in Norwell, MA.)

Letter to the Editor, Scituate Mirror, May 1974

On May 23, my son Brian and I arrived at the scene of the Cliff Hotel fire shortly after the first fire apparatus. The cool professionalism of Chief Stewart, Captain Snow, the other officers and firefighters of Scituate must be lauded and acclaimed. The courageous and exhausting efforts of these men and the firefighters of surrounding communities prevented a holocaust in Minot of terrifying dimension. The tragic loss of this historic landmark is tempered by the saving of the entire Minot section of Scituate. Well done, Scituate firefighters.

Tim McGowan, Scituate, MA

Editorial, Scituate Mirror, May 1974

The fire department did the finest job in both fighting the fire and coordinating with a whole series of mutual aid towns. Fire engines were in every driveway of every home in the area that was in possible danger.

When the alarms went out, all of the neighboring stations immediately rose to the occasion. About 200 to 250 men were at the scene. The blaze started about 9:41 p.m. on a Thursday and firemen were still there at 8:30 p.m. Friday

Firemen from Hull, Weymouth - right down the line - to Hanover and Norwell, were involved. They certainly have a system. What a fine bit of coordination and cooperation.

Inmate gets 3-5 years in Cliff Hotel Fire

Boston Globe - 1978

A Norfolk prison inmate was given a three to five year sentence yesterday for conspiring with two other men to burn down the famous Cliff Hotel in Scituate in May 1974.

Edward Glynn, 50, formerly of Quincy, was convicted on two indictments of conspiracy after a three-day trial before Judge George J. Hayer in Suffolk Superior Court. The judge ordered Glynn's sentence served after he completes two others.

Glynn, who was labeled by Roger Emanuelson, Assistant District Attorney, as a "professional criminal," has an eight year term for violation of parole to finish before he begins a 10 to 12 year sentence for another arson conviction. The Cliff Hotel, a 100-year old landmark, and a private residence located nearby were destroyed in the fire.

The key witness against Glynn was John Shaheen, 49, indicted as a co-conspirator in the case, who is now under the protective custody of District Attorney Garrett H. Byrne's office. He testified that Glynn hired him and Francis E. Pineau, 49, of Draper Street, Dorchester, to set the fire. Shaheen said they were paid $1000 for the job.

Shaheen said the three men purchased 25 five-gallon plastic jugs in South Boston and filled them with gasoline purchased at a service station on Massachusetts Avenue, Roxbury, on the day of the fire. The witness said they drove to the Cliff House where Glynn introduced them to the "owner," who was not identified in the trial. After the "owner" left the hotel, Shaheen said, he shut off the sprinkler system.

The three men returned that night and Glynn stayed in an auto parked outside, acting as the "lookout," Shaheen said, while he and Pineau spread the fuel throughout the building. Shaheen said he put two ignition devices - lighted cigarettes placed behind the heads of matches in a matchbook - on separate floors of the hotel. The resulting fire was fought by firefighters from seven communities. Seven persons residing in the house nearby narrowly escaped.

A fire insurance claim for $499,500 was filed with Massachusetts Fair Plan by Claycon Development Corp., owner of the hotel and the dwelling. On Nov. 21, 1974, the claim was settled for $434,350. However, a suit to recover the proceeds has been instituted against Claycon, whose principal officers are James Conant, 38 of Fair Oaks Lane, Cohasset, treasurer, James Claypoole, 45 of Patriot's Way, Hingham, president.

Glynn, represented by Thomas Sullivan, called no defense witnesses. The defense was based on cross-examination challenging Shaheen's credibility. Glynn, Shaheen and Pineau all were accused of involvement in the burning of a dwelling on Hilltop Street, Dorchester, on October 12, 1974. Pineau is a fugitive. Glynn received the 10 to 12 year sentence for his conviction in that case.

GLYNN SENTENCED TO PRISON TERM IN HOTEL FIRE CASE

Patriot Ledger - 1978

BOSTON - A former Quincy man was sentenced yesterday to Walpole Prison for two concurrent three-to-five year terms following his conviction Wednesday in Suffolk Superior Court for his involvement in the Cliff Hotel fire in North Scituate four years ago.

Judge George J. Hayer ordered Edward M. Glynn, 50, formerly of 81 Quarterdeck Road, to serve the prison sentence on and after an 8 year sentence for an armed robbery parole violation, which he is currently serving at Norfolk Prison, and 10 to 12 years on and after term for his arson conviction last November for a 1974 Dorchester fire.

Glynn was found guilty Wednesday of conspiracy to burn down a building and to defraud an insurer. The Cliff Hotel, a majestic hotel overlooking the ocean, was destroyed in a $340,000 blaze May 23, 1974, just prior to reopening for the summer season.

John Shaheen, 48, of Quincy, an unindicted codefendant in the case, had testified for the government that he and Francis Pineau, 49, also of Quincy, had been hired by Glynn to burn down the hotel. Negotiations for that crime were conducted in Boston, according to assistant district attorney Roger Emanuelson.

Pineau, who was indicted for the Scituate fire, fled Massachusetts shortly before his trial on charges for his involvement with the Dorchester fire.

Norfolk County Jail - 1970

3⑤

013237

3-Z

NO. 013237

Commonwealth of Massachusetts

SUFFOLK, SS.

SUPERIOR COURT FOR
CRIMINAL BUSINESS

_____August_____ Sitting, 19 77.

COMMONWEALTH

V.

EDWARD   GLYNN
FRANCIS   PINEAU
RICHARD   ROE (*James Connor*)

INDICTMENT
CONSPIRACY.

General Laws, c.   , S.

McCain—DAO

to wilfly and emolecusly set fire and burn a building

AUG 1 8 1977

Returned into said Superior Court by the Grand Jurors and ordered to be filed.

Attest:

_____ Clerk.

COMMONWEALTH OF MASSACHUSETTS

SUFFOLK, SS.   SUPERIOR COURT
                                                 NO. 013236 013237

                        COMMONWEALTH

                            V.

          RICHARD ROE. aka JAMES CONANT

          COMMONWEALTH'S MOTION TO NOLLE
                      PROSEQUI

          Now comes the Commonwealth in the above-named
case and respectfully requests that the Court enter an
order to nolle prosequi the above-numbered indictment,
for the following reasons:

          1. On August 15, 1977, one John P. Shaheen
appeared before a Suffolk County Grand Jury and described
an unknown person "in his forties, light hair, about
160 pounds" who had admitted Edward Glynn and Francis
Pineau and him into the Cliff Hotel for the purpose of
setting it on fire. The Grand Jury returned two indictments against a Richard Roe whose true name was unknown.

          2. On or about August 19, 1977, Mr. Shaheen
selected a photograph of James Conant as the person
he had described before the Grand Jury. Mr. Conant
was subsequently arrested, and plead not guilty to the
above indictments. *Oct 5, 1978 filed.*

- 2 -

3. On July 11, 1978, Mr. Shaheen testified in Suffolk Superior Court, before Hayer, J. and a jury, in the case of <u>Commonwealth</u> v. <u>Edward Glynn et al</u> (Nos. 013236-37). Mr. Shaheen stated under oath that James Conant was not the person whom he had previously described to the Grand Jury.

4. Mr. Shaheen advises the Commonwealth that in a trial against Mr. Conant, he would testify that he was not the man. The Commonwealth would have no other evidence with which to proceed against James Conant.

For the foregoing reasons, the Commonwealth respectfully moves to nolle prosequi the above-numbered indictments.

Respectfully submitted,

For the Commonwealth,

ROGER A. EMANUELSON,
Special Assistant
District Attorney

2

COMMONWEALTH OF MASSACHUSETTS

SUFFOLK, SS.   SUPERIOR COURT
                                   INDICTMENT NO.
                                   ~~013296~~

COMMONWEALTH   )   MOTION FOR PROTECTIVE ORDER
)   REGARDING PRIVILEGED MATTERS
VS.   )   PENDING BEFORE THE SUFFOLK
)   SUPERIOR COURT, CIVIL SESSION,
JAMES B. CONANT   )   JURY WAIVED

Now comes the defendant, James B. Conant, in the
above entitled indictment, and respectfully asks that
this Honorable Court issue a Protective Order that he
not be required to answer any questions in regard to the
numbered indictment and that he not be required nor the
corporation of which he was a member be required to
deliver any records before the Suffolk Superior Court,
Civil Session without a jury at a hearing for a Temporary
Restraining Order. The name of the corporation for
which a Protective Order is asked is Claycon Development
Corporation, or allow James E. Claypoole, one of two
stockholders of Claycon, to testify or present any
records of the Corporation.

                         By his Attorney:

                         Paul J. O'Rourke

Commonwealth of Massachusetts

O13937

Suffolk, ss. At the SUPERIOR COURT, begun and holden at the City of Boston, within and for the County of Suffolk, for the transaction of Criminal Business, on the first Monday of August, in the year of our Lord one thousand nine hundred and seventy-seven.

THE JURORS for the COMMONWEALTH OF MASSACHUSETTS on their oath present that

EDWARD GLYNN, FRANCIS PINEAU and RICHARD ROE, whose true name is to the said JURORS unknown, described as a white male, approximately five feet nine inches tall, with light hair and approximately forty years of age,

on divers days between the thirtieth day of April and the twenty-sixth day of May, in the year of our Lord one thousand nine hundred and seventy-four, did conspire together and with one John Shaheen to wilfully and maliciously set fire to, burn and cause to be burned a certain building, the property of Claycon Development Corporation, Inc., a corporation legally established and existing, the said building being known as the Cliff Hotel and being situated in Scituate, in Plymouth County, within the Commonwealth of Massachusetts.

And The Jurors aforesaid further say that the said John Shaheen is a co-conspirator but not a defendant in this indictment.

A TRUE BILL.

Gerald F. Muldoon
Assistant District Attorney.

William B. Dinsmore
Foreman of the Grand Jury.

FORM 235 5M 10-74

IDENTIFICATION OF JAMES CONANT AKA RICHARD ROE

On August 15, 1977, John P. Shaheen appeared before a Suffolk County Grand Jury and described an unknown person, who had admitted him to the Cliff Hotel for the purpose of setting it on fire.

On or about August 19, 1977, Mr. Shaheen was shown a group of photographs in the District Attorney's Office. He selected a photograph of James Conant, as the person who admitted him to the Cliff Hotel on May 23, 1974.

On January 23, 1978, Mr. Shaheen was shown a second group of photographs and again selected a photograph of James Conant as the person who admitted him to the Cliff Hotel on May 23, 1974.

Exhibit A

36

COMMONWEALTH OF MASSACHUSETTS

SUFFOLK, SS.

SUPERIOR COURT
INDICTMENT NOS.
013236,013237

7/11/78
Allowed
by
Agreement
Hayer. J. wke
Attest: J. Asst. Clerk

COMMONWEALTH
VS.
EDWARD GLYNN, ET AL

DEFENDANT'S MOTION TO PRODUCE

Now comes the defendant, Edward Glynn ans moves this Honorable Court to order the Commonwealth to produce certain photographs now in its possession, for the following reasons:

1. At a Grand Jury sitting, om or about August 15,1977, the Commonwealth"s witness, John Shaheen testified and gave evidence concerning facts with respect to the investigation of a fire which occurred at the Cliff Hotel, located in Scituate,Mass.on or about May 23,1974. The witness, John Shaheen testified, inter alia, that a person, whom he identified as an owner of the Cliff Hotel admitted Shaheen and one Francis Pineau into the Hotel, and described that person as, "About in his forty's,light hair,about 160 lbs., beige suit.

2. On May 15, 1978 the District Attorney's office mailed to defense counsel a certain document entitled, 'Identification of James Conant AKA Richard Roe'(a copy of which is attached hereto and marked 'Exhibit A'.

3. On July 10,1978 the District Attorney'just prior to the trial of the defendant on the above enumerated indictments handed defense counsel a letter, dated July 7.1978, which essentially set forth a recanting by the Witness Shaheen of his previous identification of James Conant AKA Richard Roe. (Exhibit "B")

2

Wherefor, the defendant says that said photographs now in
the possession of the Commonwealth, from which the witness
Shaheen previuosly identified James Conant,AKA Richard Roe
a named Co-conspirator in the above has now become an essential
element in his defense in this trial.

By defendant's attorney,

Thomas M. Sullivan
Sullivan & Cahalane
599 Pleasant Street
Brockton, Mass. 02401
Tel: 588-1222

35

COMMONWEALTH OF MASSACHUSETTS

SUFFOLK, SS.   SUPERIOR COURT
                                          NO. 013236-7

COMMONWEALTH

v.

EDWARD GLYNN, FRANCIS PINEAU
AND RICHARD ROE, AKA JAMES CONANT.

COMMONWEALTH'S MOTION FOR
DISCLOSURE OF RELIANCE ON
AN ALIBI DEFENSE.

Now comes the Commonwealth in the above-entitled
case and moves that this Court order each defendant to
disclose whether he will rely on an alibi defense, and
if so, to disclose the names, addresses and dates of
birth of all alibi witnesses.

In support of this motion, the Commonwealth states
that the defendants are charged with conspiracy to burn
a building known as the Cliff Hotel. The Commonwealth
has filed a bill of particulars stating dates and times
when each member of the conspiracy performed certain
acts in furtherance of the crime. The Commonwealth has
also provided a list of its witnesses, and will disclose
any rebuttal witnesses.

                          For the Commonwealth,

                          ROGER A. EMANUELSON
                          Special Assistant
                          District Attorney

COMMONWEALTH OF MASSACHUSETTS

SUFFOLK, SS.   SUPERIOR COURT
                                     INDICTMENT NO.
                                     ~~013236~~

COMMONWEALTH   )
)
VS.   )   AFFIDAVIT
)
JAMES B. CONANT   )

    Now comes Paul J. O'Rourke, Attorney for James B.
Conant, and states the following which he believes to
be true and accurate to the best of his knowledge and
belief.
    There is a pending Indictment, number 013236 in the
Suffolk Superior Court naming James B. Conant for conspiracy to commit arson with intent to defraud an
insurance company.
    There is also pending in Suffolk Superior Court,
Docket number 23496, a complaint against James B. Conant,
James E. Claypoole and Claycon Development Corporation,
the defendants and Massachusetts Property Insurance
Underwriting Association, the plaintiff, which has
filed a Temporary Restraining Order against the defendants.
    There will be a hearing on September 14, 1977, in
the Jury Waived Session to determine if the Temporary
Restraining Order will remain in effect and this will
require James B. Conant to file certain documents of the
Corporation, which had only two stockholders, and because
of the indictment in the Suffolk Superior Court may cause
a violation of the Fifth Amendment right of James B.
Conant of him to adequately defend himself in the Civil
suit.

                    By his Attorney:

                    Paul J. O'Rourke (signature)
                    Paul J. O'Rourke

                                    SUFFOLK SUPERIOR COURT
                                    CIVIL CLERKS OFFICE
                                    FILED

                                    SEP 14 1977

                                    MICHAEL JOSEPH DONOVAN
                                    CLERK OF COURT

        SEP 12 1977

        FILED

01323b -31

NOTICE TO PRISONERS FROM COMMISSIONER OF CORRECTION
(In accordance with G. L. Chapter 277 Sect. 72A as inserted ay Acts of 1963 Chap. 486)

To: **Edward Glynn**   N# **18380**   Date **11-30-77**   **30A**

013236;

This is to notify you that **Information (Indictments)**   identified by number **013237**

(Indictment, Complaint, Warrant, Letter

issued by the **Suffolk Superior**   Court **on 1977**   charging you with the crime(s) of

Conspiracy to Commit Arson; Conspiracy to Defraud an Insurer

has been received. Other contents, if any, of the notice about this untried offense received

from the Court are as follows: **None**   .

(Insert NONE if no additional information received)

Under the Law you have the right to apply to the Court for a prompt trial or other disposition
thereof by making application to the Court through the Commissioner of Correction. If you
choose to exercise this right, sign ALL copies of the APPLICATION TO COURT below.

APPLICATION TO COURT

To: The Honorable Justice of **Suffolk Superior**   Court.

Under the provisions of Sect. 72A Chapter 277 of the General Laws (as inserted by Chapter
486 of the Acts of 1963) I respectfully request a prompt trial or disposition of the criminal
charge(s) pending against me as described in   **Indictments (2)**   number
013236;

o **013237**   issued by your Court **on 1977**   .

Thomas Sullivan, Esq.   *Edward M. Glynn* 12-8-77
Brockton, MA   Signature of Inmate   Date

CERTIFICATE OF COMMISSIONER OF CORRECTION

I hereby certify that **Edward Glynn**   N #**18380**   now at MCI-Norfolk is serving
MCI-Walpole
a sentence of **15-20 yrs.; 9-10cc**   which he received in the **Norfolk Superior**

Court on **11-3-67**   . That he now has served approximately **10** years and **1** months of
said sentence; that there remains to be served approximately **9** years and **11** months of said
full sentence; that on his full sentence he is entitled to a deduction of approximately **6** years
and **2** months by reason of Good Conduct and/or Blood Donations; that if not earlier released
he would be given his (good conduct discharge) about **8-22-81**   , that he(is) eligible for
release on **Annual Review 8/78**   and that on his said sentence decisions of
the Parole Board have been: .

9-28-72 Parole Bd Put on 10/72 List
10-3-72 Reserve 10-10-72
10-10-72 Parole
9-12-77 Parole Revoked   *Frank A. Hall* 12-15-77
9-12-77 Returned to MCI- Walpole   Commissioner of Corrections   Date

Garrett H. Byrne
District Attorney

SUFFOLK COUNTY INVESTIGATION
AND PROSECUTION PROJECT

THOMAS E. DWYER, JR.
CHIEF COUNSEL

The Commonwealth of Massachusetts

District Attorney Suffolk District

Court House, Room 812, Pemberton Square

Boston, Massachusetts 02108

July 7, 1978

Thomas M. Sullivan, Esq.
Sullivan & Cahalane
599 Pleasant Street
Brockton, Massachusetts   02401

Re: Commonwealth v. Edward Glynn, Et Al,
     Nos. 013236-013237

Dear Mr. Sullivan:

In regards to the above-named case, please
be advised as to the following. In preparation
for trial of this case, I reviewed with the witness
John Shaheen, his identification of Richard Roe,
a co-conspirator of Mr. Glynn. Mr. Shaheen had
previously selected a photograph of James Conant
as the person referred to as Richard Roe in the
above indictments.

Mr. Shaheen informed me that he had not
seen, at the time of his original identification,
a photograph of James Claypoole. He further
informed me that, having now seen such a photograph,
he is unwilling to make a positive identification
without first having an opportunity to see James
Conant in person.

There is no doubt in Mr. Shaheen's mind
concerning his involvement with Edward Glynn and
Francis Pineau in this crime.

Very truly yours,

ROGER A. EMANUELSON,
Special Assistant
District Attorney

RAE/jcv

Exhibit B

013236
013237

COMMONWEALTH

vs.

Edward Glynn

WITNESSES WHO TESTIFIED FOR THE COMMONWEALTH

1) Walter Michael Stewart
2) Evelyn Thomas
3) James Moore
4) Richard Cotter
5) Richard Sneed
6) John Shaheen
7) Henry Mills

WITNESSES WHO TESTIFIED FOR THE DEFENDANT

JUDGE *Hayes*

ASSISTANT DISTRICT ATTORNEY *P. Emanuelson*

ATTORNEY FOR THE DEFENDANT *T. Sullivan*

CONVICTED UNDER GENERAL LAWS, CHAPTER   , s.

ACKNOWLEDGEMENTS

Memories of The Cliff Hotel was a labor of love for us ... and as the project progressed, gaining support and encouragement from individuals and organizations, we realized just how many people shared our interest in, and love for, the Cliff Hotel.

All these contributions of time, information, photographs and memories enabled us to put together what we hope is a fitting tribute to Scituate's last grand hotel.

We are especially grateful to Aram Brazilian, Jr., John Brazilian, Esq., and former SFD Deputy Chief Charles Curran who gave so generously of their time and shared so many personal and historical resources – we could not have achieved this without you! Scituate Archivist Betty Foster and the Scituate Historical Society graciously provided assistance and documents, and enthusiastic support.

We are indebted, as well, to Chief Brian Stewart, Scituate Police Department; Captain Mark Donovan, Scituate Fire Department; Chief Kevin Robinson, Marshfield Fire Department; Jessica Bartlett, Boston Globe South, and Nancy White, Editor, Scituate Mariner. All the good folks whose stories and photos helped tell the story have been acknowledged in the book's text – our sincere apologies if we left anyone out!

Special thanks to our 'technical advisors' and cheerleaders, who believed in us and kept us focused: Geraldine Lind, Paula Lind, Bailey McCallum, Tim McCallum, James Young, Richard Young, Steve Richardson, Craig Waters, Rebecca Maverick and Patte Amend. You're the best.

As mentioned in my dedication, I owe my existence to the Cliff Hotel. Beyond that, the Cliff was a constant presence in my summer landscape. I spent every summer, from the time I was three months old until I was the mother of a three-year-old, in my grandparents' cottage on Glades Road, across from the Minot Post Office. As soon as my friends and I were allowed to travel the neighborhood without supervision, we included visits to the hotel – looking for movie starts - in our daily adventures.

As teenagers, we still looked for celebrities, but spent more time hanging near the pool or in the snack bar, pining in vain after John Brazilian, the lifeguards, and some of the cute guys in the bands. I made friends with some of the young women who came from out-of-state to work at the hotel – including one gal from Kansas who had never seen the ocean.

While working on this book, the salty tang of the air or the burn of pavement on bare feet, the music floating out from the Bamboo Lounge on a soft summer night or the sheer ecstasy of a snack bar milk shake would creep into my little office, and make me feel like that kid again.

When the hotel burned down, I was in Western Mass. with my husband and little boy; by the time we returned to Scituate for a summer visit, most of the debris was gone. And that's when I realized that a special place in my youth and my heart was really gone.

Nancy Murray Young

Additional Reference Sources: bikel.com, biography.com, davidpolansky.com, imdb.com, museumtv.com, notablebiographies.com, nytimes.com, theblackpiano.com, tv.com, wikipedia.com and yale.net

CPSIA information can be obtained at www.ICGtesting.com
Printed in the USA
BVOW050848131212

307756BV00009B/5/P